Socialization to Old Age

Socialization to Old Age

IRVING ROSOW

UNIVERSITY OF CALIFORNIA PRESS
Berkeley / Los Angeles / London

University of California Press
Berkeley and Los Angeles, California

University of California Press, Ltd.
London, England

First Paperback Edition, 1977
ISBN: 0-520-03417-1
Library of Congress Catalog Card Number: 73-78540
Printed in the United States of America

1 2 3 4 5 6 7 8 9 0

To Cordy and Ben

> *whose brimming youth,*
> *in counterpoint*
> *to this book's theme,*
> *makes its dedication*
> *not an irony*
> *but a simple warrant*
> *of love*

Contents

Introduction

THIS IS a book on adult socialization theory. It is not a treatise on aging; instead, it analyzes the possible induction of elderly Americans into old age. Most changes of status in the course of life are marked by a special transition as a person leaves one social position to take up another. People finish school, join the army, marry, are promoted at work, have kids, switch jobs, get divorced, see their youngest child married, become grandparents, retire, and so on. All such changes alter a person's social identity and relationships, whether dramatically or subtly. His responsibilities and privileges invariably change and, with them, so do the standards of behavior considered appropriate to his new position.

The transmission of these standards is seldom left to chance. Whether the person enters a convent or a retirement community, the new rules are borne in on him, sometimes through formal training, but usually through informal means. The newcomer is typically familiarized with the expectations that will govern his position. In various ways he is instructed in his new obligations and rights, in the norms that are supposed to guide his conduct and relations with others, in what they can expect of him and he of them. This induction is the process of socialization.

But aging presents an unusual set of circumstances which differs from those of other socialization situations. As a result, the transition processes that typify earlier passages between age grades are aborted and fail to operate in the customary way. This is the inevitable conclusion that grows out of socialization theory. The reasons for this are the subject of this book. Its basic thesis is simple: unlike earlier status changes in American life, *people are not effectively socialized to old age.*

The problem will be examined as follows. After outlining the position of and the institutional consequences for the aged in America, differences are noted between earlier role transitions and the movement into old age. Then the central concepts of socialization and norms, with all their ambiguities, are clarified and their meaning specified in terms of the analysis presented in this book. We examine the function of norms and their critical relation to socialization criteria without which the entire concept of socialization is vitiated. A search for such criteria is made by reviewing all findings on normative expectations for the aged; this reveals that the evidence for norms is extremely weak. But because this may not be conclusive—it is possible that there are serious deficiencies in the data—the tentative results are checked for consistency with other factors of socialization. Accordingly, old people are assessed on those variables that are normally important in earlier role transitions. If the old and young correspond on these factors, the normative vacuum would be suspect; but if they differ, the evidence of weak norms would be consistent and plausible.

Thus, the major variables in socialization are closely examined, with particular attention given to the structure and elements of socialization situations, socializing agents, and formal and informal processes. There follows a review of additional factors, such as role clarity and role models, which normally facilitate socialization. Their weakness, it is found, underscores the nature of old age as a special case in which society has only a minor stake, almost certainly because of the reduced responsibilities of the aged. The general analysis shows that norms for the aged are indeed weak and that the aged are subject to only negligible socializing forces. With this conclusion, a final question is posed about possible socialization alternatives within our present institutional structure. Finally, this book postulates conditions that should be conducive to the development of roles and norms to which old people could be socialized. This theoretical proposal receives strong support from the recently published results of an independent study.

Two major caveats should be made explicit. First, in analyzing socialization we are interested in sheer age effects as such and in old people as a whole rather than in their many subgroups. We are looking at the forest, not at the trees. When referring to the norms of the aging, one obviously expects these to vary according to the older person's sex, social class, ethnicity, health, and so on—if only on the basis of their different status sets.[1] Clearly, norms for a widowed Wasp accountant and a widowed Black charwoman are different. Age does not wipe out sex, race, and class distinctions. Accordingly, old age will be considered here on the assumption that these other differences will persist. In this book, we are not interested in distinguishing various subgroups among the elderly or in making explicit all the qualifications about each. Existing data provide adequate material for such inferences, and future research can modify our basic propositions as this becomes necessary; this re-

---

1. Robert Merton, "The Role Set: Problems in Sociological Theory," *British Journal of Sociology*, 8 (1957) 106–20 and *Social Theory and Social Structure*, rev. ed. (Glencoe: Free Press, 1957) 368–84.

finement is not our immediate concern. Because it is not problematic for our analysis, we will not specify these qualifications, but we will simply assume them.

Second, in theoretical terms, aging poses a special case of socialization to a devalued status in which restitutive and social control functions are minimal. Accordingly, we do not concentrate on the usual questions about old people's happiness or "adjustment." These are perfectly legitimate issues with which I personally am much concerned. But as any mental hospital patient or prisoner fully appreciates, happiness is not intrinsic to socialization. Any group's share in the distribution of available values may be directly subject to institutional choices, and these usually encompass significant theoretical issues. But one cannot legislate "adjustment" or distribute happiness as if it were food stamps. Happiness is a function of many factors; one cannot simply decide to be happy. Accordingly, happiness is not a crucial *sociological* variable, and it is not a basic problem in this analysis.[2] The final section of the book outlines conditions that should facilitate the socialization to old age, and this question itself reflects my personal concern with the quality of people's lives and the terms of their social integration or exclusion. But this interest, too, is couched in terms of the book's central problem, consistent with its frame of reference. For any proposed institutional alternative must stand the test of theory and satisfy the factors that govern the social problem it addresses. The present caveat is important because in the area of social problems, humanitarian interests and practical questions continually subvert theoretical issues and impatiently brush aside analytic perspectives. Yet sound theory is eminently practical, though its development may

---

2. Irving Rosow, "Adjustment of the Normal Aged: Concept and Measurement," in Richard Williams, Clark Tibbitts and Wilma Donahue (eds.), *Processes of Aging*, vol, 2 (New York: Atherton Press, 1963) 195–223.

take a little time. Hence, this book must be read with a constant awareness of its theoretical concerns. While it may have many practical implications, these should be kept aside and reserved for separate consideration. In this work, we are not formally concerned with old people's happiness; instead, we are concerned with the issues of socialization which they represent.

1. *Institutional Position of the Aged*

THIS PROBLEM of old age has both practical and theoretical importance: practical because, as a growing social problem, older people affect our society and are in turn affected by it; theoretical insofar as they exemplify numerous issues of social theory, including problems of the life cycle, social roles, and adult socialization.[1]

In the interaction between the aging person and society, deprivation, dependency, and indifference impose strains on both the individual and the social order. Affluence only deepens our vexation with social problems and casts in sharp relief the controversies they evoke over the nature of our institutions, the goals of public policy, and the principles that govern the flow of equity, privilege, and honor in our society.

---

1. The analysis in this section is based upon an earlier publication, Irving Rosow, "Old Age: One Moral Dilemma of an Affluent Society," *Gerontologist*, 2 (1962) 182–91.

Older people arouse strains of social conscience. They have done the world's work and met the demands of life, only to fall prey in their later years to growing deprivation and dependence. They have not necessarily failed, so they are not personally responsible for their fate. Diffused in our midst with a quietly insistent presence, they personify uncomfortable issues of social justice. While we could resolve their problems with generosity and commitment, we have not chosen to do so. Thus, the moral dilemma they pose is of our own making and, by the same token, is within our power to dispel.

That the dilemma is one of values is abundantly clear. But this is not the entire picture. Major institutional forces are also at work which systematically undermine the position of older people in American society, depreciate their status, limit their participation, and channel them from the mainstream of social life. This is much less the case in simpler societies, but is increasingly true at an accelerating rate in modern, advanced nations. Thus, the progressive corrosion of the status of the aged is an unintended but direct result of larger social changes.

Analysis has shown that seven major institutional factors govern the status of older people in all societies. In addition to certain patterns of social organization, these concern various resources that old people command and functions they perform. The changes in modern American life have undermined these possible institutional supports and have relegated the aged to a weak position.

We can review these institutional forces briefly as background material for the ensuing analysis. We will simply summarize the broad picture in its most general terms without all the necessary qualifications and available documentation that a detailed treatment would clearly require. Here again, our concern is the forest, not the trees. With this clear caveat, the seven factors are as follows:

DETERMINATES OF STATUS

Property Ownership

Property has always been a major resource in providing the aged with security and independence. In simpler societies it also gave them substantial power over the life chances of the young and thereby a claim on their deference. But the power based on property has been weakened in the U.S. by the diffusion of ownership, the growing separation between ownership and management, and the proliferation of opportunities for the young in education and the economy. Thus, the power of the aged has been diluted at the same time that the opportunities of the young have become increasingly independent of them. Although property ownership may assure financial independence, it no longer means control over subordinate younger groups.

Strategic Knowledge

The tremendous changes—and the *rate* of change—in modern science, technology, and automation steadily depreciate the knowledge, skills, and experience that make old people respected authorities in stable societies. New knowledge and techniques develop so rapidly and are so pervasive, running the gamut from electronic computers to child rearing, that successive generations become "obsolete" at progressively younger ages. The experience of the aged tends to become irrelevant and to count for less and less as radically new specialties and concepts become established. The old even lose their special qualification to instruct the young, who are increasingly trained by formal education and indoctrinated with attitudes and values by middle-age parents, the mass media, and their peers. Thereby the aged have no special claim to cultural authority and are regarded neither as strategic teachers and models nor as respected founts of wisdom by younger groups.

Productivity

The aged can preserve their social functions longest in low-productivity economies. Primitive technology with limited production tends to preserve the marginal utility of successive increments of labor. Although labor may be cheap, low productivity creates opportunities and functions for old people who are still able to add to the small gross product. But our economy is inordinately productive, and our problem is to maintain demand, not supply. The growth of technology and automation has generally eliminated labor shortages except in certain professions and special labor categories. Old people do not particularly command those new skills which are in short supply. Therefore, with high productivity and no general labor scarcity, their marginal utility in the labor force tends to be low. They have relatively poor employment prospects once they are out of work because their contribution to the economy is not highly valued.

Mutual Dependence

High productivity has raised living standards and private resources; economic growth and governmental subsidies have also increased opportunities and personal autonomy. These have strengthened individual independence and self-sufficiency, thereby reducing people's reliance on others for help. This weakens mutual obligation and the constraints of reciprocity. As a result, the necessity of personal cooperation has declined, and the solidarity of mutual dependence has been undermined.[2] Self-concern has increased at the expense

---

2. For an analysis of how proliferating opportunities may weaken primary group ties, see Irving Rosow, "Affluence, Reciprocity and Solidary Bonds," paper prepared for the Biennial Meeting of the International Society for the Study of Behavioral Development: Ann Arbor, August, 1973 (publication pending).

of group solidarity. Thus, prosperity and autonomy have weakened the informal mutual aid networks that have traditionally been the most important mechanisms for meeting the needs of older people. In a mass society, responsibility for them is becoming increasingly formalized, ritualized, and depersonalized as a public problem.[3]

Tradition and Religion

In contrast to tradition-bound simpler cultures, we are an innovating society strongly dedicated to "progress." We have only a very limited heritage that present generations carry on and to which the aged are a meaningful link. Our predominant values are materialistic and secular rather than sacred, future- rather than past-oriented, and pragmatic rather than traditional. Hence, older people are not a viable symbol of historical continuity and respected tradition. Certainly they provide no religious ties to the gods, as they do in cultures with ancestor worship, such as the classical Chinese. Thus, social change militates against the traditional orientations that engender respect for the aged.

Kinship and Family

Our present family structure has fragmented the multi-generation family and the kinship network that typified pre-industrial times. Such organized reciprocal obligations among relatives specifically included old people and respected their needs. But the modern occupational system has put a premium on smaller, mobile families, and these have become the norm. In this context, with increasing resi-

---

3. Indeed, the steady shift of responsibility for aged parents from their children to the state has been stimulated by the courts in rulings that establish the prior claims of adult children's self-advancement over the needs of their parents. See Alvin Schorr, *Filial Responsibility in the Modern American Family* (Washington: Social Security Administration, 1960).

dential separation of different generations, obligations are ranked in a hierarchy of priority which leaves older people disadvantaged in comparison with younger generations.[4]

Community Life

The division of labor and specialized roles underlying modern urban life have weakened those stable local community structures that effectively integrate older people in a broad range of age groups. This loosening of ties has been

---

4. Cf. Talcott Parsons, "Revised Analytical Approach to the Theory of Social Stratification," in Reinhard Bendix and Seymour Lipset (eds.), *Class, Status and Power* (Glencoe: Free Press, 1953) 92–128; "The Social Structure of the Family," in Ruth Anshen (ed.), *The Family: Its Function and Destiny* (New York: Harpers, 1949) 173–201. On the other hand, Eugene Litwak argues that the modern extended family retains significant cohesion, viability and mutual aid, even in the face of major geographic and social mobility ("Geographic Mobility and Extended Family Cohesion," *American Sociological Review*, 25 [1960] 385–94). Aside from important weaknesses which may be criticized in the sample at Litwak's disposal, he focuses on family solidarity in meeting sundry crises, such as major illness or financial aid in securing a child's college education. While this may be true, this is drastically different from the cohesion which develops from continued proximity. Sustained daily interaction results in viable group living and integration of older people in family groups, as opposed to the intermittent help to overcome emergencies. Indeed, Peter Townsend finds that in the face of intergenerational occupational and social mobility, the meaningful emotional ties between generations in a family become strained, ritualized and atrophied in contrast to the sustained solidarity when mobility does not disrupt family structure and interaction (*Family Life of Old People* [London: Routledge and Kegan Paul, 1957]). And social contact and interaction are indispensable to morale (Bernard Kutner, *et al. Five Hundred Over Sixty* [New York: Russell Sage, 1956]; Sheldon Tobin and Bernice Neugarten, "Life Satisfaction and Social Interaction in the Aging," *Journal of Gerontology*, 16 [1961] 344–46). Townsend's evidence sharply contradicts Litwak's case. The entire problem is quite subtle and difficult to resolve without careful research that can cut through ritualistic behavior to establish its significance for the participants. Recent work, however, has clearly called into question the extreme formulations of Parsons on the extent of nuclear family isolation within larger kinship networks. See the Duke University symposium on this problem: Ethel Shanas and Gordon Streib (eds.), *Social Structure and the Family: Generational Relations* (Englewood Cliffs, N.J.: Prentice-Hall, 1965).

intensified by residential mobility, changing neighborhoods, and the common impersonality of urban environments. Consequently, local group life tends to be limited, ephemeral, and superficial rather than pervasive, durable, and binding. Hence, people's most significant associates commonly live outside their local neighborhoods.[5] But insofar as people's local dependencies increase as they age and their mobility is reduced, the purely local institutions tend to accommodate them poorly.[6]

In summary, the institutional forces that typically support the position of old people in simpler societies are inimical to them in our own. Paradoxically, our productivity is too high and our mutual dependence too low. We are too wealthy as a nation and too self-sufficient as individuals to need older people, and the significant social functions open to them are shrinking. This both reflects and reinforces other established cultural values, such as our greater concern for the young and our general youth-orientation.

CONSEQUENCES FOR OLDER PEOPLE

Devaluation

The consequences of these institutional patterns are clearly marked. First, the aged are generally devalued.[7] This

---

5. Joel Smith, William Form and Gregory Stone, "Local Intimacy in a Middle-Sized City," *American Journal of Sociology*, 60 (1954) 276–84.

6. Wendell Bell and Marion Boat, "Urban Neighborhoods and Informal Social Relations," *American Journal of Sociology*, 62 (1957) 391–98; Irving Rosow, "Retirement Housing and Social Integration," *Gerontologist*, 1 (1961) 85–91, also in Clark Tibbitts and Wilma Donahue (eds.), *Social and Psychological Aspects of Aging* (New York: Columbia University Press, 1962) 327–40; Joel Smith, William Form and Gregory Stone, *op. cit.*

7. Milton Barron, "Minority Group Characteristics of the Aged in American Society," *Journal of Gerontology*, 8 (1953) 447–82; Raphael Ginzberg, "The Negative Attitude toward the Elderly," *Geriatics*, 7 (1952) 297–302; Peggy Golde and Nathan Kogan, "A Sentence Comple-

is reflected in younger groups' negative attitudes, relative
indifference to, or even rejection of the elderly. Their basic
devaluation and its concomitants are absolutely basic factors
in their prospective socialization to old age. We shall presently consider this.

Stereotyping

Second, they are commonly viewed in stereotypes, as
are other devalued minority groups. Thus, they are seen
more as representatives of an age group than as individuals,
and various negative characteristics are attributed to them.[8]
Significantly, these images of the old are not confined to
younger people alone, but are also widely shared by the
aged themselves.[9] Old persons depreciate other aged persons,

tion Procedure for Assessing Attitudes toward Old People," *Journal of
Gerontology*, 14 (1959) 355–63; Bertram Hutchinson, *Old People in a
Modern Australian Community* (Carlton, Australia: Melbourne Univer-
sity Press, 1954); Maurice Linden, "Effects of Social Attitudes on the
Mental Health of the Aging," *Geriatrics*, 12 (1957) 109–14; Joost Meerloo,
"Some Psychological Problems of the Aged Patient," *New York State
Journal of Medicine*, 58 (1959) 3810–14.

8. Joseph Drake, "Some Factors Influencing Students' Attitudes
toward Older People," *Social Forces*, 35 (1957) 266–71; Raphael Ginzberg, *op. cit.*; Joost Meerloo, *op. cit.*; Jacob Tuckman and Irving Lorge,
" 'When Aging Begins' and Stereotypes about Aging," *Journal of Gerontology*, 8 (1953) 489–92.

9. Milton Barron, *op. cit.*; Robert Havighurst and Ruth Albrecht,
Older People (New York: Longmans & Green, 1953); Nathan Kogan,
"Attitudes toward Old People in an Older Sample," *Journal of Abnormal
and Social Psychology*, 62 (1961) 616–22; Nathan Kogan and Michael
Wallach, "Age Changes in Values and Attitudes," *Journal of Gerontology*,
16 (1961) 272–80; Bernice Neugarten and David Garron, "The Attitudes
of Middle-Aged Persons Toward Growing Older," *Geriatrics*, 14 (1959)
21–24; Jacob Tuckman and Irving Lorge, "Attitudes toward Older Workers," *Journal of Applied Psychology*, 36 (1952) 149–53 and "Old People's
Appraisal of Adjustment over the Life Span," *Journal of Personality*, 22
(1953–54) 417–22; Jacob Tuckman, Irving Lorge and G. A. Spooner, "The
Effect of Family Environment on Attitudes toward Old People and the
Older Worker," *Journal of Social Psychology*, 38 (1953) 207–18; Irving
Zola, "Feelings About Age Among Older People," *Journal of Gerontology*,
17 (1962) 65–68.

and in the same terms. Furthermore, these images of older people do not vary according to others' direct contact or experience with them, but tend to be fairly stable, regardless of exposure.[10] Hence, the stereotyped conceptions are not easily subject to change through direct association.

Exclusion

Third, the aged are excluded from equal opportunities for social participation and rewards enjoyed by younger members of their social class, ethnic, or racial group.[11] To this extent, they become relatively disadvantaged in the later years and lose significant bases of their earlier social integration.

Role Loss

Fourth, not the least of such attrition is their role losses.[12] This constitutes a conspicuous alienation from major family and work roles: through widowhood and retirement, through the damage to symbolic life styles from lower income after retirement, and through the general decline in

---

10. Joseph Drake, *op. cit.*

11. Wilma Donahue, Harold Orbach and Otto Pollak, "Retirement: The Emerging Social Pattern," in Clark Tibbitts (ed.), *Handbook of Social Gerontology* (Chicago: University of Chicago Press, 1960) 330–406; Margaret Gordon, "Aging and Income Security," in Clark Tibbitts (ed.) *op. cit.*, 208–60, "The Older Worker and Hiring Practices," *Monthly Labor Review*, 82 (1959) 1198–1205, and "Work and Patterns of Retirement," in Robert Kleemeier (ed.), *Aging and Leisure* (New York: Oxford University Press, 1961), 15–53; William Harlan, "Meaning of Economic Security to Older Persons," *Transactions of the Illinois State Academy of Science*, 44 (1951) 182–86; Irving Rosow, "Old Age: One Moral Dilemma of an Affluent Society"; Harold Sheppard, "Unemployment Experiences of Older Workers," *Geriatrics*, 15 (1960) 430–33.

12. Bernard Phillips, "A Role Theory Approach to Adjustment in Old Age," *American Sociological Review*, 22 (1957) 212–17; K. W. Schaie, "The Effect of Age on a Scale of Social Responsibility," *Journal of Social Psychology*, 50 (1959) 221–24.

health, which can impair sheer independence. Except for a minority who are disengaged, the loss of roles is mainly involuntary and unwelcome, even when illness forces retirement.[13] Role losses inevitably affect previous group memberships, lower prestige, and reduce one's status sets and the social integration that they provide the individual. We will return to this presently.

Role Ambiguity

Fifth, role loss entails a sharp reduction of responsibility and a limitation of function, the net result of which is role ambiguity. There is comparatively little prescribed activity that attends old age. The role tends to be open, flexible, and unstructured.[14] It may be defined with a maximum of personal preference and individual choice. This seeming boon, however, calls heavily on people's initiative and inner resources in the absence of definite role expectations by others.[15] Such negative demands are not always easily met and may generate as much strain as do conflicting role pres-

---

13. Benjamin S. Prasad, "The Retirement Postulate of the Disengagement Theory," *Gerontologist*, 4 (1964) 20–23; Herbert Rusalem, "Deterrents to Vocational Disengagement Among Older Disabled Workers," *Gerontologist*, 3 (1963) 64–68.

14. Robert Havighurst, "Flexibility and the Social Roles of the Retired," *American Journal of Sociology*, 59 (1954) 309–11; Robert Havighurst and Ruth Albrecht, *op. cit.*; Aaron Lipman, "Role Conceptions and Morale of Couples in Retirement," *Journal of Gerontology*, 16 (1961) 267–71; Harold Orbach and David Shaw, "Social Participation and the Role of the Aging," *Geriatrics*, 12 (1957) 241–46; William Smith, Joseph Britten and Jean Britten, *Relations within Three-Generation Families*, Research Publication 155 (University Park, Pennsylvania: Pennsylvania State University, College of Home Economics, 1958); Richard Williams "Changing Status, Roles and Relationships," in Clark Tibbitts (ed.), *Handbook of Social Gerontology* (Chicago: University of Chicago Press, 1960) 261–97.

15. Woodrow Hunter and Helen Maurice, *Older People Tell Their Story* (Ann Arbor: University of Michigan, Division of Gerontology, 1953); Bertram Hutchinson, *op. cit.*

sures.[16] Indeed, role loss and ambiguity are generally quite demoralizing; they deprive people of their social identity and frequently affect their psychological stability.[17] The apparent freedom is often a burden because earlier in life, roles typically structured expectations, requirements, and activities for them.[18] Most workaday routines do not result from intention, but merely from occupying a particular social position and from several decisions at crucial points in the life cycle. The unstructured situations of later life are inherently depressing and anxiety-generating. Older people must fill the vacuum of social expectations with personal definitions, and they must develop private standards in the absence of established norms for them. Many of the elderly respond to their devaluation and ambiguous role by clinging to youthful norms as a means of dealing with the new uncertainties.

Youthful Self-Images

Finally, older people also cling to youthful self-images. Or, as Bernard Baruch expressed it, "To me old age is always fifteen years older than I am." One of the most consistent findings of surveys of old people is their refusal to acknowledge that they are old.[19] Most of them claim that they con-

16. Leonard Cottrell, "Adjustment of the Individual to his Age and Sex Roles," *American Sociological Review*, 7 (1942) 617–20; Arnold Rose, *Theory and Method in the Social Sciences* (Minneapolis: University of Minnesota Press, 1954).

17. Alfred Heilbrun and Charles Lair, "Decreased Role Consistency in the Aged: Implications for Behavioral Pathology," *Journal of Gerontology*, 19 (1964) 325–29; Louis Leveen and David Priver, "Significance of Role Playing in the Aged Person," *Geriatrics*, 18 (1963) 57–63.

18. Leonard Goodstein, "Personal Adjustment Factors and Retirement," *Geriatrics*, 17 (1962) 41–45.

19. Milton Barron, "The Dynamics of Occupational Roles and Health in Old Age," in John Anderson (ed.), *Psychological Aspects of Aging* (Washington: American Psychological Association, 1956) 236–39; Zena Blau, "Changes in Status and Age Identification," *American Sociological Review*, 21 (1956) 198–203; Bernard Kutner, *et al., op. cit.*; Evelyn

sider themselves as middle-aged or young.[20] And the older they are, the later they think that "old age" begins.[21] This indicates a deep and widening split between older people's self-images and the conceptions that others have of them. Indeed, the discrepancy between these perspectives and old people's self-images inevitably creates a strain. Nonetheless, it reflects how much the aged accept the larger views and values of their society. We will also return to this presently.

In summary, the position of the elderly has several consequences: they are devalued, viewed in invidious stereotypes, excluded from social opportunities; and they lose roles, confront severe role ambiguity in later life, and struggle to preserve self-esteem through youthful self-images.

Mason, "Some Correlates of Self-Judgments of the Aged," *Journal of Gerontology*, 9 (1954) 324–37, and "Some Factors in Self-Judgments," *Journal of Clinical Psychology*, 10 (1954) 336–40; Bernice Neugarten and David Garron, *op. cit.*; S. Payne, "The Cleveland Survey of Retired Men," *Personnel Psychology*, 6 (1953) 81–110; Jacob Tuckman and Martha Lavell, "Self-Classification as Old or Not Old," *Geriatrics*, 12 (1957) 661–71; Jacob Tuckman and Irving Lorge, "Classification of the Self as Young, Middle-Aged or Old," *Geriatrics*, 9 (1954) 534–36; Jacob Tuckman, Irving Lorge and F. Zeman, "The Self-Image in Aging," *Journal of Genetic Psychology*, 99 (1961) 317–21; Irving Zola, *op. cit.*

20. Such youthful self-images are reflected in choices that people make in identifying themselves as young, middle-aged or old. These responses indicate preferences on an implicit value scale where they accept society's youth orientation and the valuation of youthfulness. This may well be similar to the dilemmas of choice of identity and reference groups exhibited by other marginal groups. For example, light skinned Blacks often had the option of living as Blacks or of "passing" as white. It is an old story that in various self-assignments, whether on social class position or power in small groups, people tend to upgrade themselves in relation to assignments that others make of them. That is, they describe themselves as closer to the preferred social norm than others describe them. And in their youthful self-images, older people also accept and reflect the dominant social norms about age.

21. Raymond Kuhlen and Everett Luther, "A Study of the Cultural Definition of Prime of Life, Middle Age, and of Attitudes toward the Old," *Journal of Gerontology*, 4 (1949) 324; Woodrow Morris, "Age Attitudes and Health," *Adding Life to Years*, 8 (March, 1961) 3–6; Jacob Tuckman and Irving Lorge, "'When Aging Begins' and Stereotypes about Aging," *op. cit.*, and "When Does Old Age Begin and a Worker Become Old?" *Journal of Gerontology*, 8 (1953) 483–88.

2. The Life Cycle
and Status Sequences

GERONTOLOGISTS sometimes gloat with assumed wisdom over the paradox that aging literally starts at the moment of conception (or, for conservatives, at the moment of birth). But this is a socially meaningless statement. In addition to ignoring the difference between growth and decline, it confuses physiological condition with social position, which has differing norms and expectations. While it is important for geriatricians to develop objective measures of relative physical "age," these would have no *social* meaning unless they were highly correlated with the behavior of older people and with that of others toward them. Yet we know that this relationship is not strong. There are large individual differences in physical health which make for significant discrepancies between chronological and "functional" age. At the same time, despite minor variations between social classes, the onset of "social old age" tends to be fairly stable and uniform. It tends to creep up unobtrusively during the middle and later fifties, so that people tend to be regarded as socially "older" from somewhere near the age of sixty.[1] Their actual treatment does not vary significantly with individual differences in health and capacity until these become extreme. Hence, sociological rather than objective physical factors primarily govern the social definitions of old age.

In this sense, old age represents the last stage in the sequence of age-sex roles in the life span.[2] Each stage is commonly recognized and identifiable, if not always with great precision. Each has its own set of norms and expectations which taken together comprise an age-sex role. Accordingly, each has its distinctive pattern of activity, responsibility, authority, and privilege which varies from that of other stages. For example, the propriety of a young wife's working is judged by different standards if she has an infant or is childless.

Such status sequences may be identified in various institutional areas and described in different ways. For example, career profiles might be developed for top executives or other subgroups in the labor force. In this case, however, the profiles would represent mobility ladders that could be completely traversed only by the most successful minority. The majority would only encompass portions of these successive statuses. Thus, in academia, one young instructor might rise to associate professor by the time he retired, while another might go through all the professorial ranks through department head, deanship and even a college presidency.

---

1. Bernice Neugarten and Warren Peterson, "A Study of the American Age-Grade System," *Fourth Congress of the International Association of Gerontology,* vol. III (Fidenza, Italy: Tito Mattioli, 1957), 497–502; Jacob Tuckman and Irving Lorge, " 'When Aging Begins' and Stereotypes about Aging," *Journal of Gerontology,* 8 (1953) 489–92, and "When Does Old Age Begin and a Worker Become Old?" *Journal of Gerontology,* 8 (1953) 483–88.

2. Paul Glick, "The Family Cycle," *American Sociological Review,* 12 (1947) 164–74.

Obviously such sequences are not confined to the occupational world. Similar successions can be identified in the family and elsewhere: most persons eventually move through all family levels.

The critical factor in stages of the life cycle is the identification of basic age-sex roles that are traversed in their *entirety* by *most* of the population, if not by all—such as those who die young or never marry. Different frameworks might vary from one another in detail, in refinement of levels, in the timing of given successions for different social classes, and so on. But even with such qualifications, we may suggest one typical sequence of life-cycle stages which most people can normally expect to cover completely, taking on the entire series of new roles. Thus, one succession of age-statuses might include the following profile:

Infancy: preschool years
Childhood: school years
Adolescence: sexual maturation
Young Adulthood: completion of education and start
                              of work
Marriage
Parenthood: establish family
Middle Age: raise family
Grandparenthood
Old Age: especially stigmata of widowhood, retirement, illness, and senility

Clearly, variations on this theme are possible, and additional stages might well be interpolated—for example, the period of courtship and engagement, or the period of family contraction when adult children have finally left home. These would embellish or refine the series without affecting the basic notion. In the normal course of events, most adults may expect to go through this entire progression of roles. This is implicit in the very concept of life cycle.

PROPERTIES OF ROLE TRANSITION

In this process, the movement from one role to another has several important properties. However, these characteristics apply almost exclusively to role successions *before old age* and only rarely to the movement *into* old age. This distinction has important consequences, which will be discussed later. At this point we will briefly review three significant properties of transition from one life stage to the next.

Rites of Passage

First, the most important status changes are often observed by public ritual—*les rites de passage*—or by private ceremonials among those most affected by the change. Baptism, initiation or confirmation rites, college graduation, the marriage ceremony, and funeral all formalize leaving one status behind and acquiring a new one.[3] The primary referent is always the actor himself, and the secondary referents extend to collaterals. Such ceremonies signal the revision of ties within the role set. Baptism of a first child or grandchild not only installs and locates a new member, but also formalizes the new family that has come into being and the new roles of parent and grandparent, and changes their reciprocal obligations to each other. These observances of role transition have several functions for the actor and the group. They (a) socially redefine the person publicly, (b) symbolize his status change, and thereby (c) facilitate his passage from one definite position to another.

Social Gains

Second, status successions almost invariably involve net social gains. The person typically moves from one position

---

3. Arnold Van Gennep, *Rites of Passage* (Chicago: University of Chicago Press, 1960).

of lower responsibility and prerogatives to another where both are increased. He also passes from states of dependence to independence and then to positions where he supervises or manages others who are socially less skilled or competent—typically younger persons. Thus, in an occupational prototype, for example, he may progressively move from learning to practicing to teaching to administrating to policy making. By these moves, the person takes on greater responsibility and autonomy and exercises more leadership and authority. Thus, successive positions usually involve social gains.

Again, however, this does not mean that all adults attain equal power or eminence in all spheres. On the contrary, only a minority achieve critically strategic social positions. Nor are all gains equally steady and uninterrupted; some peak early and level off while others are sustained.

But for the average person, the overall profile of status succession is one of gain and acquisition. His share of available values tends to increase with his movement through the sequence of age-sex roles. His sphere of decision is larger, his prerogatives and rewards are greater, the number of people over whom he exercises authority is larger while the number exerting authority over him is smaller, and he has greater recognition. These gains are specifically *age-related*. They are independent of any other rewards, such as those underlying social mobility. The sheer transition from one stage of the life cycle to the next systematically increases the person's prerogatives in accordance with his greater social maturity and competence.

The basis of these greater rewards is crucial. *They are a function of meeting increased social responsibility.* Childhood, adolescence, young adulthood, marriage, and parenthood progressively extend a person's responsibilities. At the youngest ages, these focus on the person himself, so that a child is expected to learn and acquire skills that reduce his dependence and the care he requires. With greater independence, he is gradually expected to assume more responsibility for himself and eventually for others. These expectations are inherent in growing up and are integral to age roles. Because successive ages entail growing responsibility, they are accorded greater authority. Similarly, because meeting these obligations is socially *consequential*, society provides a system of incentives and prerogatives. Thus, as with other roles, differential rewards to age groups are based on increasing responsibility and the potential consequences of role performance.

This pattern applies quite generally to status transitions *before* old age—with one possible exception. Movement into grandparenthood presents some ambiguity. The social gains are not so clear-cut and unambiguous. Direct responsibility may increase, but not significantly. Correlatively, regardless of any psychological pleasure, the social rewards do not grow appreciably, if at all.[4] Quite apart from any satisfaction deriving from grandchildren themselves, the life stage of grandparents is one of easing burdens of heavy family responsibility and increased opportunities for sheer self-indulgence. The relief from obligations occurs when many other major social functions are still retained, social participation is high, rewards and resources are substantial if not at their very maximum, and there is the greatest opportunity simply to enjoy life.[5] Resources, opportunity, and desires are in the most favorable combination. Hence, even though increments of authority and prestige are not so great on becoming a grandparent as in earlier role transitions, the possibilities for

---

4. The personal gratifications may even operate as functional substitutes for social rewards. While not literally functions of grandparenthood per se, they are certainly correlates of that life stage.

5. Irving Rosow, "Adjustment of the Normal Aged: Concept and Measurement," in Richard Williams, Clark Tibbitts and Wilma Donahue (eds.), *Processes of Aging*, vol. 2 (New York: Atherton Press, 1963) 195–223.

sheer fun and gratification may be significant personal substitutes for status increases. However, the slowdown in social gains at this stage is a harbinger of the reversals and actual losses that mark the impending transition to old age, but without adequate preparation for it.

Role Continuity

Third, the last property of status successions to be considered here is role continuity. This refers to the expectations in one role that positively prepare a person for the next position or at least impose no norms that actively conflict with those of the next stage. Thus, continuity represents similar standards in two successive periods or at least no inconsistencies which impose distinctive strains on role transitions. In terms of Ruth Benedict's classic discussion of the problem, continuity implies that training in one phase: (a) fits a person for later conventions, (b) does not pervasively taboo behavior that is later required or permitted, (c) does not induce one behavior while requiring an opposite one later, and (d) does not have to be unlearned later on.[6] To the extent that sequential norms are compatible in these terms, there is continuity between roles. In ideal form, this becomes direct anticipation of and active preparation for the future role. The contrary pattern—conflicting or inconsistent standards, norm reversal, and unlearning—represents role *discontinuity*. Thus, continuity refers to the smoothness of passage between life stages so that earlier expectations are no obstacle to later adaptation, and they provide the core onto which later norms are grafted. Continuity thereby represents a consistent extension rather than a revision of age norms.

We can illustrate the concepts of role continuity and discontinuity in life-stage transitions by examining the effect

6. Ruth Benedict, "Continuities and Discontinuities in Cultural Conditioning," *Psychiatry*, I (1938) 161–67.

of education in preparing boys and girls for their adult sex roles. The immediate focus is occupational, but the basic principles are general to all role sequences.

In the growth to adulthood, the completion of school and the movement into full-time work are marked by continuity for men. All levels of the educational system prepare the boy for the next level of schooling. The American educational system has long been devoted to occupational training. This typifies public schools and most higher education, including undergraduate and graduate liberal arts programs as well as professional schools. Hence, education is directly geared to the occupational system and effectively services it. To this extent, education is essentially vocational and trains young people for future employment. This includes their being indoctrinated with attitudes and values that employers regard as appropriate.[7] And criteria for judging occupational performance are basically extensions of educational standards to a new sphere. Therefore, the transition from school to work exemplifies role continuity for men.

But this period of life shows major discontinuities for women.[8] By and large, the educational system makes no significant distinction between the training of girls and boys. Schools are coeducational from the start, the bulk of students pursue the same course of studies, they cultivate the same sets of skills, the same requirements are made of them, the same standards are used to judge and rate them, and they have similar rewards and comparable access to positions of prestige and honor—with minor concessions to sex differences, such as athletic participation, manual training as opposed to

---

7. Howard Becker, *et al.*, *Boys in White* (Chicago: University of Chicago Press, 1961); Robert Merton, George Reader and Patricia Kendall, *The Student-Physician* (Cambridge: Harvard University Press, 1957); Howard Vollmer and Donald Mills (eds.), *Professionalization* (Englewood Cliffs, N.J.: Prentice-Hall, 1966).

8. Mirra Komarovsky, "Cultural Contradictions and Sex Roles," *American Journal of Sociology*, 52 (1946) 184–89.

home economics on the periphery of the program, etc. This similarity of training obtains throughout the educational system.

The schools are sensitively geared to future occupational positions of men, but not to different adult sex roles, especially in marriage. On the completion of education, men and women enter the labor force to face significant *inequalities* of opportunity and reward for similar work. Women still confront systematic and pervasive discrimination, which does not need documentation. Then, after marriage, and especially after the birth of children, the burden of domestic responsibility falls on them. Despite the recent trends in the family toward blurring the division of labor between the sexes, the primary responsibility for the home and children still rests on the wife.[9] Yet her education does not prepare her either for job discrimination or housewifery. On the contrary, her training develops skills for the labor market and cultivates achievement values, but conspicuously neglects any preparation for domesticity. Hence, when women complete education or leave the labor force to care for a home and raise a family, they experience a drastic shift in activity and norms. Thereby, marriage and motherhood tend to impose strong role discontinuity.

In summary, the sequence of childhood and adult statuses *before* old age generally functions with role continuity. The most conspicuous exception is the preparation of girls for married life. But aside from this, transitions from one life stage to the next are *not* distinguished by major inconsistencies, reversal or unlearning of previous norms. There tends to be coherent preparation, development, and extension of basic expectations from one age level to the next.

---

9. For an analysis of this problem and a proposal for a fundamental equalitarian family, see Alice Rossi, "Equality between the Sexes: An Immodest Proposal," *Daedalus*, 93 (1964) 607–52.

THE TRANSITION TO OLD AGE

But this is not the complete picture, for a different pattern crystallizes in aging. These major properties of role transition simply do not apply to growing old; the movement into later life assumes another form.

No Rites of Passage

First, rites of passage occur primarily on earlier occasions, but seldom in the later years. Except for the occasional retirement dinner and the obvious stigmata of aging, such as entering a nursing home, old age tends to develop gradually and informally. Subtle changes in relationships, group memberships, and participation are typical. These often *follow* rather than precede other people's redefinition of the person as aging or old. The only fairly abrupt and clear changes are retirement, widowhood, and institutionalization. These usually arise *after* the redefinition has occurred and symbolically validate it. They confirm rather than initiate *social* old age. Others' attitudes and treatment of the elderly person alter, often without his immediate awareness. In the main, people become socially old by drifting into it rather than through sharply punctuated events. Hence, a formal *rite de passage* seldom occurs, and, except for the funerals of widowhood, there are few public observances of a status change.

To this extent, aging, like dying, represents what Glazer and Strauss term a "non-scheduled status passage."[10] It is not a specific event that is scheduled in advance, such as starting school or reaching voting age. Rather, it is an in-

---

10. Barney Glaser and Anselm Strauss, "Temporal Aspects of Dying as a Non-Scheduled Status Passage," *American Journal of Sociology*, 71 (1965) 48–59.

evitable, but vague and unregulated process. Such indefinite status successions pose their own special problems:[11]

> For the non-scheduled status passage, the important questions are how the occupant in passage, as well as those people around him, even know in the first place *when* he ... is in movement between statuses. Further, how do these people define the succession of transitional statuses, ... where the next transition will take him, and how the occupant is to act and be treated by others at various points in the passage? Also, what happens when the occupant in the passage and those around him have *different perceptions* ..., and what kinds of interaction are consequent upon these different perceptions? When differential perceptions [exist], interaction strategies to handle these issues become crucial.

Such differential perceptions that are not corrected by a *rite de passage* or by some other means underscore the central problem of ambiguous norms for the aged.

Social Losses

Second, old age is the only stage in the life cycle that has systematic social losses rather than gains. The major life tasks are basically finished, responsibility declines, and dependency may increase. There is severe alienation from central social roles through widowhood and retirement; a loss of rewards from drastic declines in income, which is reduced by more than 50 percent after retirement;[12] and a mounting curve of illness and physical handicap. These losses and their correlates of dependency, isolation, and demoralization in-

---

11. *Ibid.*

12. Leonore Epstein, "The Income Position of the Aged," in Harold Orbach and Clark Tibbitts (eds.), *Aging and the Economy* (Ann Arbor: University of Michigan Press, 1963) 91–102; Lloyd Saville, "Flexible Retirement," in Juanita Kreps (ed.), *Employment, Income and Retirement Problems of the Aged* (Durham: Duke University Press, 1963) 140–77; *Impact of Inflation on Retired Persons*, National Advisory Committee, White House Conference on Aging (Washington: 1960).

crease progressively in the later years. After the mid-seventies, they grow at a steeply rising rate with each successive year. Taken together, they indicate older people's sharply reduced social participation and greater marginality. The entire basis of their social integration is weakened, and the advantages of active social roles and group memberships glimmer away. Accordingly, becoming old inevitably reflects a loss of responsibility and the prerogatives that go with it. Society attaches little importance to the older person's functions and thereby accords him less than a pro rata share in the distribution of rewards.

Obviously, the position of the aged is not undermined equally in all societies, nor is this fate inevitably a function of pure physical decline. Rather this varies with the social structure and the meaning with which old age is invested.[13] Under some conditions, particularly in nonindustrial societies, older persons are not only valued, but they do not face significant status loss. Certain cultures, as in rural Ireland, protect the position of the elderly.[14] In others, old age, though not senility, is largely honored and respected, as it was in classical China.[15] In these stable, traditional societies, the place of the person in the social order is protected not only by his economic functions, but also by his production of *noneconomic* values. These may have important religious, aesthetic, symbolic or other functions that the old are peculiarly qualified to fulfill. Hence, old age is not universally a stage of social decline. But in America the highest rewards are provided for the creation of economic utility. Furthermore, the

---

13. Irving Rosow, "Old Age: One Moral Dilemma of an Affluent Society," *Gerontologist*, 2 (1962) 182–91; Leo Simmons, *The Role of the Aged in Primitive Society* (New Haven: Yale University Press, 1945), and "Social Participation of the Aged in Different Cultures," *Annals*, 279 (1952) 43–51.

14. Conrad Arensberg and Solon Kimball, *Family and Community in Ireland* (Cambridge: Harvard University Press, 1940).

15. Albert Chandler, "The Traditional Chinese Attitude toward Old Age," *Journal of Gerontology*, 4 (1949) 239–44.

American's *present*, not his past activity mainly governs the current evaluation of him. Past performance is only limited collateral for short-term credit in the competitive status market.[16] And, as we have seen, social and technological changes steadily produce earlier obsolescence and thereby restrict the basis of status claims after middle age. Hence, old age becomes a period of social decrement and loss.

This does not mean that there are no major social losses with other status changes. Actually, there is a wide variety of these. Getting divorced, becoming widowed at a young age, being crippled, having an illegitimate child, failing in business, becoming a criminal, being an alien refugee, or slipping downward in occupation or social class also represent significant declines in status. But these changes are not typical and affect only minorities of the population. They figure in actuarial expectations and life chances, with low incidence rates for the population as a whole. They do not involve the majority who go through life without facing such status decrements. Hence, they differ from old age, whose losses are the inevitable fate of virtually everybody who survives long enough. While some people do face various status declines (often from social class hazards), old people suffer them as a sheer consequence of survival.

Role Discontinuity

Finally, the movement into old age is marked by sharp role discontinuity, especially for men. The culture does not significantly prepare a person for becoming old or obsolete or for losses. Middle-age experience does not "train" people for an aged position or for new standards in later life. There

---

16. Irving Rosow, "Retirement Leisure and Social Status," in Duke University Council on Aging and Human Development, *Proceedings of Seminars, 1965–1969* (Durham, N.C.: Duke University Center for the Study of Aging and Human Development, 1969) 249–57.

is no regular effort to clarify a prospective style of life that would be appropriate, even though anticipatory attitudes are vital to subsequent adaptations.[17]

Indeed, the entire subject tends to be ignored except in the genuflection of preretirement counseling programs. These are not widespread,[18] and, with few exceptions, they tend to be extremely limited and superficial, lasting an hour or so between one and five times during the five years before retirement, usually in the last few months. These meetings are almost completely devoted to information and plans on retirement income plus a bit of vague advice to find a hobby and remain active. Further, they tend to have little effect unless the worker already has a positive attitude toward retirement and looks forward to it, often because of poor health.[19] But virtually nothing is done to prepare the worker for a distinctive retirement role and to help him find meaningful substitutes for work. Hence, after the early glow of lounging in bed for a few weeks rather than going to work, the retiree is faced with the problem of fashioning for himself within and outside the household a new role to structure his life and activities.[20]

For women, the transition is usually not so abrupt, for their domestic responsibility tapers off over a longer

---

17. Wayne Thompson, "Pre-Retirement Anticipation and Adjustment in Retirement," *Journal of Social Issues*, 14, No. 2 (1958) 35–45; Wayne Thompson and Gordon Streib, "Situational Determinants: Health and Economic Deprivation in Retirement," *Journal of Social Issues*, 14, No. 2 (1958) 18–34; Wayne Thompson, Gordon Streib and John Kosa, "The Effect of Retirement on Personal Adjustment: A Panel Analysis," *Journal of Gerontology*, 15 (1960) 165–69.

18. Wayne Thompson, *op. cit.*

19. *Ibid.*

20. Woodrow Hunter and Helen Maurice, *Older People Tell their Story* (Ann Arbor: University of Michigan, Division of Gerontology, 1953); Aaron Lipman, "Role Conceptions and Morale of Couples in Retirement," *Journal of Gerontology*, 16 (1961) 267–71; S. Payne, "The Cleveland Survey of Retired Men," *Personnel Psychology*, 6 (1953) 81–110; Gordon Streib, "Morale of the Retired," *Social Problems*, 3 (1956) 270–76.

period, beginning with the time when adult children begin to leave home for education, work, or marriage. Hence, women can adapt to their declining role more slowly, in less abrupt stages.[21] Further, after sixty-five, most women are widowed; they are widowed at twice the rate of men for any given age before the mid-eighties. However, there is comparatively little to prepare women (or men) specifically for widowhood and the drastic financial and social changes that will confront them. Also, neither men nor women are prepared for the dependency imposed by the inevitable losses of income and health.

In general, old people must learn from their own experience and adapt by themselves. The culture does little to help in their transition to old age or with the many problems they then face for the first time: alienation from central roles, loss of status and respect, increasing marginality, and the withering of social participation. There are virtually no prior role prescriptions other than bromides to stay active and to maintain independence.

In summary, the transition to old age differs significantly from earlier status successions. Its occurrence tends to be vague, amorphous, and unregulated, as the scarcity of its *rites de passage* effectively reflects. The movement into old age involves major *social losses*, including central roles and their responsibility, authority and rewards. Finally, there is basic *role discontinuity*, with no preparation for such losses and no substitution of new norms, responsibilities, and rights. These conditions have profound implications for the prospective socialization to old age which we will presently examine.

---

21. An equivalent "phasing-out" retirement program for men has been experimentally introduced in several firms. Instead of complete and abrupt retirement, work is gradually reduced over a three to five year period. Men move from full-time employment through progressive stages of part-time work, perhaps starting with a three-fourths work week and moving toward one-fourth time or less. Such programs seem to offer relatively successful transitions to retirement and permit a gradual adjustment to it, similar to the gradual domestic tapering-off of women.

3. *Theoretical Preface*

AXES OF SOCIAL INTEGRATION: THE CONTEXT OF THE PROBLEM

WE SHOULD briefly indicate the relation between socialization and social integration, or how individuals are tied into the social order. Social integration locates persons in a system and patterns their relationship to others. It may be conceived from two standpoints: (1) The system, or how subsystems are articulated with one another, and (2) the member, or how individuals function within the system. Our focus is on the individual. The general categories or referents of socialization and integration are the same, so that socialization becomes one major mechanism of integration.

The integration of individuals can be analyzed in terms of three sets of distinct, but linked factors:

A. Social Values
B. Social Roles
C. Group Memberships
    1. Formal Organizations
    2. Informal Groups, Friendships, etc.

These provide the ties that bind social norms into institutions, structure social intercourse, place a person in society and order his relation to others. Thereby, they provide the means and substance of integration. Other categories of social identity, such as ascribed statuses or social class, are expressed and function through these factors.

Within this framework, how do these patterns of integration change with increased age?[1] (A) On social values, there is little evidence that older people's beliefs differ significantly from those of younger persons specifically *as a function of aging*. This applies not only to basic **social values** that the old have assimilated as well as the young, but even to social perceptions.[2] Nor does any evidence clearly support such stereotypes about the aged as their putative growing religiosity[3] and increasing political conservatism.[4] Differences among age groups are explicable as a function of historical experience rather than of aging *per se*.[5] Therefore, the elderly remain essentially integrated in society in terms of their values and beliefs. (B) As has been indicated earlier, aging clearly involves the inevitable loss of central **social**

1. This section summarizes an intensive analysis of recent research and other relevant literature in Irving Rosow, *Social Integration of the Aged* (New York: Free Press, 1967), esp. pp. 8–30.

2. Peter Blau, "Occupational Bias and Mobility," *American Sociological Review*, 22 (1957) 392–99; Nathan Kogan and Michael Wallach, "Age Changes in Values and Attitudes," *Journal of Gerontology*, 16 (1961) 272–80.

3. Elaine Cumming and William Henry, *Growing Old* (New York: Basic Books, 1961); Harold Orbach, "Aging and Religion," *Geriatrics*, 16 (1961) 530–40.

4. William Evan, "Cohort Analysis of Survey Data," *Public Opinion Quarterly*, 23 (1959) 63–72; Irving Lorge and K. Helfant, "The Independence of Chronological Age and Sociopolitical Attitudes," *Journal of Abnormal and Social Psychology*, 48 (1953) 598; Otto Pollak, "Conservatism in Later Maturity and Old Age," *American Sociological Review*, 8 (1943) 175–79.

5. Seymour Lipset, *et al.*, "The Psychology of Voting," in Gardner Lindzey (ed.), *Handbook of Social Psychology*, vol. 2 (Cambridge: Addison-Wesley Press, 1954) 1124–75. Also, cf. Irving Rosow, *Social Integration of the Aged*, pp. 10–13.

roles and their correlates, notably in marriage, work, income, health, the family, and so on. (C) Finally, **group memberships** also decline drastically with age. Membership in formal organizations is primarily a function of social class position and of identification with the local community.[6] But within these conditions, participation drops off sharply with increased age,[7] membership becoming passive or lapsing. Similarly, friendships and informal associations wither away from isolation, migration, illness, or death.[8]

In summary, there is virtually no loss of old people's integration on the basis of their values, but there are major losses of social roles and group memberships. Generally, role loss is largely inevitable and irreversible. Most of the decrement is accounted for by retirement, widowhood, and failing health. These are seldom reversed, and there is little potential for their recovery. The clear decline in group memberships is equally important for reduced integration.[9] But loss of mem-

---

6. Howard Freeman, Edwin Novak and Leo Reeder, "Correlates of Membership in Voluntary Associations," *American Sociological Review*, 22 (1957) 528–33.

7. Wendell Bell and Maryanne Force, "Urban Neighborhood Types and Participation in Formal Associations," *American Sociological Review*, 21 (1956) 25–34; John Foskett, "Social Structure and Social Participation," *American Sociological Review*, 20 (1955) 431–38; Robert Havighurst, "The Leisure Activities of the Middle-Aged," *American Journal of Sociology*, 63 (1957) 152–62; Arnold Rose, "The Impact of Aging on Voluntary Associations," in Clark Tibbitts (ed.), *Handbook of Social Gerontology* (Chicago: University of Chicago Press, 1960) 666–97; Charles Wright and Herbert Hyman, "Voluntary Association Memberships of American Adults: Evidence from National Sample Surveys," *American Sociological Review*, 23 (1958) 292–93.

8. Zena Blau, "Changes in Status and Age Identification," *American Sociological Review*, 21 (1956) 198–203; Bernard Kutner, *et al.*, *Five Hundred Over Sixty* (New York: Russell Sage, 1956).

9. Morris Axelrod, "Urban Structure and Social Participation," *American Sociological Review*, 21 (1956) 13–18; Zena Blau, "Changes in Status and Age Identification," *op. cit.*; Ernest Burgess, "Social Relations, Activities and Personal Adjustment," *American Journal of Sociology*, 59 (1954) 352–60; Ruth Cavan, "Family Life and Family Substitutes in Old Age," *American Sociological Review*, 14 (1949) 71–83; Bertram Hutchinson, *Old People in a Modern Australian Community* (Carlton, Australia:

berships, though problematic, may be more amenable than that of roles to arrest or reversal. This possibility should not be arbitrarily precluded. We will subsequently consider friendship groups as a potential focus of socialization to old age.

It is beyond the scope of this book to elaborate a general theory of adult socialization. But we will examine in the context of aging several factors in earlier status successions that are drawn from a more comprehensive analysis of adult socialization.[10]

SOCIALIZATION DEFINED

First, what do we mean by socialization? We may define it in the following terms:[11]

Adult socialization is the process of inculcating new values and behavior appropriate to adult positions and group memberships. These changes are normally internalized in the course of induction or training procedures, whether formal or informal. They result in new images, expectations, skills, and norms as the person defines himself and as others view him. Thus, there are both internal and external changes: within the individual, in his role set and in the interaction between them. . . .

Socialization standards are drawn from the norms of a given target system: a specific *role*, a *group*, or the *values*

Melbourne University Press, 1954); Bernard Kutner, *et al., op. cit.*; Dell Lebo, "Some Factors Said to Make for Happiness in Old Age," *Journal of Clinical Psychology*, 9 (1953) 385–90; Martin Martel, "Family and Friendship Patterns of Older Iowans," *Adding Life to Years*, 8 (July, 1961) 3–6; Sheldon Tobin and Bernice Neugarten, "Life Satisfaction and Social Interaction in the Aging," *Journal of Gerontology*, 16 (1961) 344–46; Peter Townsend, *Family Life of Old People* (London: Routledge & Kegan Paul, 1957).

10. Irving Rosow, "Situational Forces in Adult Socialization" (unpublished manuscript).

11. Irving Rosow, "Forms and Functions of Adult Socialization," *Social Forces*, 44 (1965) 35–45.

of broader social categories. Successful socialization produces conformity to *shared* expectations about values and behavior. But regardless of the target system, socialization always has the same objectives: to inculcate in the novice both values *and* behavior, or beliefs and action. Our basic premise is that conformity is invariably sought on *both* dimensions; all socialization processes are directed to these twin ends. In any context, the fully socialized person internalizes the correct beliefs and displays the appropriate behavior.

Clearly, however, . . . the process does not function like a social die press which stamps out uniform social products. Socialization results do vary, and deviance may result from many causes.

When socialization is successful, the person generally assimilates new conceptions that include new norms, behavior patterns, and self-images. In this way, there may be a reorganization of his motives and goals as well as a modification of his standards of judgment and propriety for himself. These changes are internal and touch various levels of the personality. Effective internalization maximizes *voluntary commitment* to the new standards and minimizes the need for special incentives and controls to secure desired behavior. Thereby, the person accepts and conforms to social expectations so that the requirements of a system are translated into personal motives and goals that guide activity.[12] Consequently, a socialized individual can ". . . sustain interaction with someone other than the agents of his immediate socialization. If he can do this, society provides him with a conventional code of rules for interaction. . . . Socialization, then, is a preparation for *social performance* of the individual actor."[13]

---

12. David Aberle, *et al.,* "The Functional Prerequisites of a Society," *Ethics,* 9 (1950) 100–11.

13. Ernest Becker, "Socialization, Command of Performance, and Mental Illness," *American Journal of Sociology,* 67 (1962) 494–501.

This process applies to any social system regardless of its character or moral value. It refers to one mechanism of system maintenance. This does not preclude the possibility of deviant behavior patterns, including the distinctive forms of dissent or protest that precede social change.[14] Nor does it preclude individual differences. The terms and nuances of performance may be colored by a person's life history or modified by aspects of his personality. So, in any role, there is some range of acceptable leeway in motivation and behavior, in the style, quality, or degree of commitment.[15] But aside from innovative deviance and personal elements, there are always limits to acceptable variations that reduce the possible strains of dissidence. By and large, some minimal level of agreement about proper norms and role expectations is necessary to support the viability of any system. This minimum is initially sought through the socialization of its members and then is sustained through other mechanisms that combine routine incentives and controls.

Clearly, the criteria of successful socialization cannot be confined to the *dominant* definitions of the larger society. People are also effectively socialized to the deviant values of subcultures and marginal groups. The central issue is not their content, but simply *whether* beliefs are adopted. Thereby people may be systematically socialized to deviant values. The crucial factor is the relationship of the person to his group and its socializing agents and his absorption of their norms. So long as he internalizes the beliefs and conforms to the shared expectations, he is socialized. That the socialization may involve deviant values is another matter, for the socializing processes within his reference group have been effective.

---

14. Robert Merton, *Social Theory and Social Structure*, rev. ed. (Glencoe: Free Press, 1957), esp. pp. 131–94.

15. Nelson Foote, "Identification as the Basis for a Theory of Motivation," *American Sociological Review*, 16 (1951) 14–21.

He is observing the group standards. While his compliance may vary within limits, conformity itself is intrinsic to the very concept of socialization.

Thus, successful socialization secures the *voluntary* conformity to some set of *shared* expectations and norms. Members take on the basic standards of their society or groups in regard to a role. Socialization becomes a major mechanism to place people in social positions, to pattern their relationships with others, and to inculcate those values that govern action and support the system. Thereby, roles are fulfilled acceptably, and the system's necessary work is carried out in a relatively stable, predictable manner.

PSYCHOLOGY OF SOCIALIZATION

Two basic psychological conditions seem necessary for socialization to a given role. First, the person must see the role and its associated values as *legitimate* in a system to which he belongs or aspires to belong.[16] Secondly, he must personally *identify* with the role so that his access to it seems proper to him. Thereby, its norms are not simply impersonal features of the social landscape, but are also appropriate for him. This relates the person to the new position in terms of his own status sequences.[17]

The future position may be in the same role set as his present one and thereby complement it. This can be seen in the identification of a son with his father in the family or of a graduate student with his professor in a university. To the son and the student, the father and the professor represent possible future states for themselves. But people do not always aspire to such a complementary position in their role set, in which case this does not become their goal. They do not

---

16. Melvin Tumin, "Rewards and Task-Orientations," *American Sociological Review*, 20 (1955) 419–23.
17. Robert Merton, *op. cit.*, pp. 368–84.

personally identify with the position. Actors commonly define goals in static or negative terms, often as a reflection of how others in the role set affect them. Accordingly, they see themselves and their place in the system in limited perspective. Without aspirations, routine relationships tend to ossify and restrict future expectations. This may characterize persons who have risen to the highest *subordinate* position that they want or can reach in a group or organization, and it may well be intrinsic to the status quo pressures in bureaucracies.

On the other hand, other members of a role set *do* aspire to higher complementary positions in that set. Their view of these roles is usually dynamic and flexible, they identify with them, and they probably adopt the incumbent perspective quite readily.[18] Thus, such an aspirant may invest the future position with wider, deeper meanings than a nonaspirant. For example, conceptions of parental roles crystallize during childhood and adolescence when children usually take their own future marriage and parenthood for granted. Also, during World War II, career army officers from West Point probably had more sensitive awareness than their OCS colleagues of pressures upon and alternatives open to their superior officers. This awareness is intrinsic to the process of *anticipatory socialization* in which a person becomes receptive to and often learns some of the attitudes and values of a given position or group *before* he actually becomes a member. This is stimulated, certainly at the cognitive level, when both positions are within a single role set. However, regardless of its roots, *the critical socialization factor is personal identification with a role*.[19] Without identification, the potential for socialization is drastically limited and presents special problems.

---

18. Walter Coutu, "Role-Playing vs. Role-Taking," *American Sociological Review*, 16 (1951) 180–87; Ralph Turner, "Role-Taking, Role Standpoint and Reference Group Behavior," *American Journal of Sociology*, 61 (1956) 316–28.

19. Nelson Foote, *op. cit.*

Such identification is one of the three subjective steps that comprise the psychological elements of socialization: (1) **cathexis** of the *role;* (2) **identification** with a real or ideal role *model;* and (3) **introjection** of the role model's *values.* These occur at personality levels where the most basic changes and consolidation of self-images take place; and changing self-conceptions are intrinsic to socialization. Without all three components—cathexis, identification, and introjection—socialization tends to be deficient, so that the person lacks belief in or commitment to the role, and its norms are problematic for him. Cathexis of the role and identification with a model may occur in any sequence, so that either step can come first or both can develop together. Once in process, they interact to reinforce each other.

But, conceptually, there can be no significant socialization to a group or role without the internalization of norms.[20] Indeed, introjection represents the crucial closure of any socialization cycle. It signifies that new values, standards, and expectations have been incorporated in the self and are associated with observable behavioral changes. To this extent, introjection is the crux of socialization, while cathexis and identification are its antecedent conditions.

Naturally, these three subjective elements are unconscious mechanisms that the person is typically unaware of. But even if he does not perceive them directly, the actor is usually aware of their effects. Thus, socialization involves the normal processes of emergent self-conceptions discussed by Cooley, Dewey, Mead and more recent students of symbolic interaction, role-taking, and reference group theory,[21] in-

---

20. This does not mean that roles cannot be *performed* without introjection of values or that values cannot be assimilated without taking on a new status. Both are possible and have their place in a typology of socialization (Irving Rosow, "Forms and Functions of Adult Socialization"). But, from a conceptual standpoint, full socialization involves both *performing* a role and *internalizing* its values.

21. Erving Goffman, *The Presentation of Self in Everyday Life*

cluding the social structural emphasis supplied by Merton and Rossi.[22] It is apparent, then, that regardless of the person's awareness of his own psychological operation, we are not dealing here with a sheer mechanistic process, as, for example, in conditioning theory. Considerably more voluntarism is involved than appears in various reinforcement theories: more reference group selection, more influence of significant others, and more effects of previous experience. In other words, social factors are significant.

While psychological processes are involved in socialization, *they are not our primary focus.* Our concern is with the *social* factors in the acquisition of new roles and the changes in values, behavior and self-images that attend it. For our purposes, we are treating the psychological mechanisms as a black-box phenomenon while concentrating on the social inputs and products. This will be a sociological analysis, not a psychological one.

(New York: Anchor Books, 1959); Anselm Strauss, "Transformations of Identity," in Arnold Rose (ed.), *Human Behavior and Social Processes* (Boston: Houghton Mifflin, 1962) 67–71; Ralph Turner, *op. cit.*

22. Robert Merton and Alice Rossi, "Contributions to the Theory of Reference Group Behavior," in Robert Merton and Paul Lazarsfeld (eds.), *Continuities in Social Research: Studies in the Scope and Method of "The American Soldier"* (Glencoe: Free Press, 1950) 40–105.

4. *Norms in Socialization*

THE BASIC function of socialization is the transmission and inculcation of social norms. Yet the concept of norms can be elusive and ambiguous, fraught with different meanings and usage that confuse and interfere with communication. This is especially true in dealing with the issues of adult socialization. The many vagaries and implicit connotations of the term introduce serious misunderstanding to a problem area that is already overloaded with subtlety and complexity. To avoid this, we must set forth our basic premises about the concept and relate them to aging. Accordingly, this section will clarify our main assumptions about norms and indicate how the term will be used in this analysis.

MEANING OF NORMS

As a general reminder, the term norms usually has one of three different meanings: clinical, statistical, or social. The **clinical** simply refers to criteria of medical or psychological health or illness. These may affect, but cannot in themselves determine, general social standards for aged roles. They may set the conditions for social expectations, but they do not define them. Therefore, clinical norms are not problematic here, and they are not our present concern. Any possible confusion involves the other two meanings.

The **statistical** norms represent various modal group characteristics. They summarize the statistical properties of a group in terms of frequencies, rates, distributions, and profiles on given factors, including those suitable for actuarial tables and future projections. In other words, statistical norms establish the central tendencies of a population on selected attributes.

To this extent, they are purely *descriptive*, not evaluative; they tell us what is, but not what ought to be. Sheer statistical standards are not value specifications and provide no basis for judging whether the features they describe are good or bad, desirable or undesirable, prized or shunned. For example, most old women are widowed, and this is the inevitable statistical fate of most American women. Also, most of the aged are poor; after retirement or widowhood, drastic income declines are the sheer statistical fate of most old people. But it does not follow from either of these facts that widowhood or poverty is valued and sought. The clearest statistical standards do not necessarily reflect people's attitudes toward the conditions they portray. In other words, *statistical norms are not social norms*.

In contrast, **social** norms do express preferences and value judgments. Basically they are normative standards of desired values and activity; in the present case, of what is regarded as appropriate to an aged role. In this sense, social norms govern the specifications of a role and the standards by which behavior is judged. Therefore, social norms are primarily *evaluative*, not descriptive; they tell us first what should be, not simply or necessarily what is.

Once stated, the simple distinction between statistical and social norms is so painfully obvious as to make any discussion of it embarrassing. Yet after acknowledging the formal distinction, many readers unwittingly forget the difference and treat the two as synonymous. Equating the two is fostered whenever a statistical modality is *also* highly valued, as, for example, the good functional health of most older people. But not all modalities are prized. As the incidence of widowhood reminds us, there is no assurance that any characteristic is valued simply because it predominates. For any given factor, the statistical and normative values must be established separately. In the most common form of error, then, sheer statistical modalities are uncritically assumed to be valued. But to equate these different norms casually is to confuse issues in a way that makes the meaningful analysis of socialization impossible. Despite its painful obviousness, we cannot emphasize this caveat strongly enough: *statistical modalities are not social norms*. This distinction must be borne in mind because the present analysis is focused on social norms.

LOCUS OF NORMS

As a second major premise, we are concerned with the social norms of old age that are defined by the culture. If norms are understandings that are shared and if socialization is their means of transmission, the scope of consensus is important. Norms may be relatively private and confined to small groups, such as families, small work teams, and so on. To this extent, though they are viable within their field, they may be quite idiosyncratic and highly variable between fields. They are social, but limited and local; they are shared, but not widely.

However, aging is a broad, pervasive social process that is societal in scope. Any meaningful consideration of age norms, therefore, must start with this large frame of reference in order to identify widely shared definitions. Such norms do not have to be universal, and few are, but they should be broadly based in large segments of society. For then many people would have similar expectations about what is appropriate for the aged, even though these might vary somewhat among major sectors of the system. In this sense, they resemble norms about social class, sex, race, or similar statuses that are shared by significantly large numbers of persons. When people become old, this certainly does not eliminate the age factor in role relationships. In other words, to examine *general* normative expectations, we cannot simply address the private or local definitions in families, other primary groups, or organizations. We must examine what is common and shared across institutional contexts. It is a problem in consensus.

Ultimately we shall be concerned with the local definitions. As we shall see, common social norms are quite weak. In the face of this semivacuum, possible local standards (or the conditions favorable to them) represent a significant theoretical alternative. But we must first examine norms in a broader social context.

ROLE RELATEDNESS

Normative expectations vary greatly in relation to particular roles, and old age underscores the special importance of three aspects of norms, their: (1) *moral force*, (2) *specificity-generality*, and (3) *explicitness*. We will consider each of them briefly.

Moral Force

In any role, the constraints on the actor differ in moral force. Generally, the requirements of him vary from situations of high moral pressure, with few behavioral options, to those of low pressure, with many alternatives. Hence, norms may refer to beliefs or actions that are *proscribed, prescribed, preferred* or *permitted*.[1] The variation is basically structural, and what is expected of the actor may be specific, limited and compelling, or broad, vague, and mild. Clearly, the most imperative moral force is associated with various proscriptive and prescriptive norms. These are typically invoked for the strongest and most central values, the situations of greatest urgency, and those involving the most consequential decisions or responsibility for others.

But older persons do not occupy many crucial positions, and the scope of their responsibility for others has dwindled drastically. Consequently, we should expect relatively few prescribed norms in old age. But this leaves open the prospects of proscribed, preferred, and permitted standards. Within the constraints of health and income, aging should be attended by fewer normative requirements and more options than earlier adult life stages. In any case, the possible expectations about older people remain to be studied in terms of their moral force.

Specificity-Generality

Norms also vary in their specificity and generality. To have any analytic meaning, norms must be formulated in terms of specific roles, no matter how broad these may be. That is, they must clearly apply to a particular role or series of roles as reference points. Insofar as age expectations do structure one's life, activity, and relationships, these norms must minimally refer to a definite life stage, no matter how vaguely conceived or how differentiated within that stage. To repeat our earlier caveat, this makes full allowance for any further refinement within the age factor, such as sex distinctions and so on, so that different norms may govern old men and old women. So long as norms contain an age component, they are

---

1. Robert Merton, *Social Theory and Social Structure*, rev. ed. (Glencoe: Free Press, 1957) 133.

role-specific for our purposes. But if they cannot be related to the age variable, they become meaningless for the problem. Certainly in this sense, norms must be *age-specific* (or stage-specific).

But this obvious requirement does not exhaust the problem of generality in assigning norms. For in order to abstract the norms that are specific to a role, it is necessary to distinguish those that are peculiar to it from those that are common to several roles that a person has. This involves how the norms of any new role are related to those of other roles in the person's status set. In this sense, the actor's various positions set the context for the transmission of new norms, so that socialization ultimately involves the problem of integrating multiple roles. In other words, multiple roles complicate the issue of normative specificity.

The problem must take account of two different kinds of relationships between a person's roles. In one, the roles are (a) *independent*; in the other they are (b) stratified or *nested*.

(a) **Independent** roles are those that are separate and distinct, but on the same analytic level. Though they coexist, they are independent of each other in the sense that one does *not* systematically *require* or imply another. Thus, one may be a plumber, father, Catholic, Southerner, Republican, member of a bowling team or bridge club, and so on. Several might even be highly intercorrelated, but there is no structural imperative that they be so. Any given status does not arbitrarily presuppose or preclude another. Thereby, the roles are relatively independent, and there are many "degrees of freedom" in their combinations and mixes. Though there may be a good deal of consistency among their respective norms, this is not always the case. Indeed, the requirements of many positions can create strong role conflicts, even when the sheer substance of the norms is compatible. However, in such status sets, presumably the norms for any role can be specified independently of the others. This should certainly be true for old age in any given social context.

Despite this independence, reconciling the norms of new and old roles presents three basic issues. The first is the possibility of *role conflict*, and this is seldom prevented or minimized. For the socializing system tends to follow one of three procedures: to ignore or deny the conflict; to acknowledge it, but make no provision for its resolution, simply allowing the person to wallow in and be buffeted by it to find his own solution; and to establish some priority of conflicting claims, some guidelines to indicate which norm takes precedence under given conditions. The third alternative assures no viable solution because the competing institutional groups may have different sets of priorities that simply aggravate the strain. Indeed, in most conflicts those in each sphere insist on the priority of its claims at the expense of the person's other obligations, and the actor is caught in the middle. Hence, the clear specification of norms in socialization, however desirable, is no guarantee against conflicting demands. But as far as the aged are concerned, their situation consists much more of rolelessness than of incompatible expectations. So the sheer fact of their multiple roles should not be particularly problematic.

The related second issue is the extent to which *values external* to a role set may affect the norms of an incumbent of a given position. Goode argues that this is possible because commitments to *roles* may be low, while commitments to significant *persons* may be high. Thereby, possible value conflicts may be resolved in favor of personal loyalty rather than of status obligations.[2] This seems to be particularly relevant to the situation of the elderly, whose status obligations decline sharply while their children and other significant intimates

---

2. William Goode, "Norm Commitment and Conformity to Role-Status Obligations," *American Journal of Sociology*, 66 (1960) 246–58.

remain. But this is misleading, for Goode is concerned with the resolution of conflicting demands. Obviously there is no problem when two sets of expectations coincide, and it is only problematic when they differ. Such situations may arise under various conditions, for example: when particularistic ties are stronger than universalistic, when internal role conflict or larger social conflicts divide the role set or the status set, or when general social change poses alternatives that eventually affect specific role expectations. In the framework of socialization theory, this problem essentially takes the form of conflicting reference groups and can be treated accordingly. But, as we have suggested, this is not particularly germane to the socialization to old age. Normative ambiguity does not arise because of value conflicts that invade the status set to confuse the appropriate expectations about an older person. Rather, as we have indicated, confusion inheres in the sheer weakness and limitation of norms. Under these conditions, adaptation may follow Goode's pattern. Personal ties and the encouragement of private preferences may be highly supportive of the old person and help to structure a role for him. But to the extent that these private definitions are unshared outside the primary group, they are no substitute for more *general* social norms and expectations in the socialization to old age.

Aside from possible role conflicts, the third issue in taking on a new role is the *adaptation* of its norms to the others in the person's status set. A given role may well have specific norms, but these are seldom absolute and inflexible. They are typically mediated by and interpreted in relation to a person's other statuses, so that expectations are adjusted accordingly. This does not imply any drastic changes, but simply acknowledges the particular context in which the new role is embedded. By this token, a new age status does not preclude existing statuses. But any specific new norms at this stage of life will be modified and adapted in accordance with the person's other roles. On this basis, age-specific norms should take into account not only the older person's sex, but also his race, ethnicity, family position, and so on. This should follow the same processes by which marital norms are related to a person's social class and occupation. This procedure is simply taken for granted as a latent assumption of much, though definitely not all, socialization: other statuses are treated as a set of constants that qualify new norms. But this modification does not reach the specificity of expectations which can be quite explicit and refer to a single role. Hence, age norms are not mutually exclusive with other standards. Therefore, any consideration of norms for older people must proceed on the assumptions that age itself does not preclude other statuses and that age norms are adjusted accordingly.

(b) Beyond the relationship between independent roles is that between stratified or **nested** roles. This involves positions that are organized in a hierarchy so that each one is subsumed under another above it. In this sense, the roles are stacked, each nesting within a higher one. Because the higher subsumes the lower and furnishes some of its general premises, there is a significant overlap in their norms. But because the higher is not actually part of the lower and the overlap is undefined, the specificity of norms becomes blurred.

In these levels, the norms of the higher tend to be more inclusive, broader in scope, and more general, while those below are more limited and specialized. In any culture, the most general values tend to be universal, while the most specific are closely linked to specialized positions. Thereby, the more widespread values usually occur at the more inclusive levels, but they also cover many of the more limited segments that they encompass on lower levels. Accordingly, when values at one level subsume norms on another, the flow of influence is downward, from the broad sphere to the sphere of narrower range.

We can illustrate these levels of generality in the following example. Here, each successive category of the social system is more limited than, and subsumed under, the one above. Lawyers are professionals of the middle class in our society; thus, as one moves down from more general to more restricted levels, the scope of the norm contracts:

Institutional Level	Ideal Norm
Cultural Universal	Justice should be based on laws, not men.
Middle Class	Honest people should be equitable and respect each other's legitimate rights.
All Professions	Personal information about clients should be privileged and confidential.
Lawyers	Litigation should always be avoided if differences can be reasonably composed.

Thus, the broader the institutional scope, the more inclusive the norm; conversely, the more specific the role, the more limited the norm. In this example, the cultural, social class, and professional norms all apply to lawyers. However, the constraint on gratuitous litigation is specific to lawyers. But it is *not* particularly binding for any nonlawyers. Other professionals, middle-class nonprofessionals, or American working-class persons may have an unbridled appetite for litigation without being guilty of *normative* deviance—poor judgment, perhaps; but deviance, no.

Of more immediate importance is the implicit "nesting" assumption: members of the legal profession have presumably absorbed a large range of norms from all the higher levels —cultural, social class, and professional. Lawyers are expected to respect basic conceptions in the larger society, such as those incorporated in the Bill of Rights; to adhere to middle-class codes of dress, speech, demeanor, and conduct; and to observe ethics and principles that presumably distinguish the professions from different occupational groups, including others of their social class. In this sense, the lawyer's role is predicated on a set of expectations or ground rules derived from more inclusive statuses within which his position is located. This is the nesting principle.

Thus, the specific norms governing narrower or more specialized roles commonly presuppose many values of higher institutional levels. These are *objectively* neither integral to the role nor necessary to it. But because they are part of its larger social context, they are usually assimilated in the pattern of role expectations. For example, professional people have traditionally been expected to display middle-class manners and deportment, but not because these are role-specific or taught in the legal curriculum. They have been implicit in professional norms as part of the *educated* middle-class life style. The rationale for them in professional expectations is that they were regarded as integral to the social context, as part of the social prerequisites, somewhat analogous to academic qualifications. And, as with academic qualifications, it was assumed that these would be acquired prior to professional school or, if not, at least would be made good independently of the curriculum. Such middle-class standards that are superimposed on strictly technical professional requirements illustrate the distinction that Max Weber drew between substantive and formal rationality, the former representing the larger value nexus that the purely objective considerations should respect.[3]

Possible strains between substantive and formal rationality are latent in nested roles, and they leave somewhat ambiguous our requirement of role-specific norms. For they pose the problem of whether contextual norms are indeed specific. In a practical sense, there may be no difficulty when there is a stable correspondence of social class and professional standards. Then these higher norms can be assumed, if

---

3. Max Weber, *Theory of Economic and Social Organization* (New York: Oxford University Press, 1947).

somewhat adventitiously. They can be conceptualized as secondary and classified at an intermediate or lower level in the hierarchy of moral force, possibly as preferred norms. This would do no violence to normative specificity. But this is contingent on a basic *consensus* about such expectations.

However, this does not solve the general issue of contextual norms. A problem does arise when the necessary consensus is lacking, when there is a challenge to the legitimacy of imposing middle-class standards that are *not objectively* germane to the role. This situation is far from hypothetical, as virtually any beleaguered professional school faculty in the country can eloquently testify. In the new generation of professional students, the winds of social change have challenged these traditional values. Nor can these differences be equated with other value conflicts within a profession, for these are typically role-specific in their focus. What is in dispute at this point is precisely the crux of the analytical problem—the role-specificity of the norms themselves, or in contemporary parlance, their relevance. Under these circumstances, if they are not formally rational and their very legitimacy is being challenged, what is the status of such nested norms in relation to role specificity? Until the problem can be analyzed significantly beyond this point, any interim conceptual resolution must remain arbitrary.

Despite the strains of change, most nested norms do not reflect social conflict, for it is a more general problem. They are attached to a particular role not because of its special characteristics, but only by virtue of linking several positions on different levels. How this can be reconciled with the requirement of normative specificity remains to be clarified. This will depend on a more refined analysis of the hierarchy of norms than is afforded by our variable of moral force. But the issue of role-specificity of nested norms—and to a lesser extent, those of independent roles—remains a vital unresolved problem of socialization theory.

However, in terms of the aged, multiple roles should pose no major difficulty. In the formulation of norms for the elderly, independent status sets should be more significant than nested roles. This should allow for a reasonably flexible adaptation of possible norms to particular circumstances of old persons. This does not mean that old age should be summarily dismissed as a nested role, only that the possibility warrants further consideration before being rejected.

Explicitness

Beyond the factors of moral force and specificity-generality, the third major aspect of norms concerns their explicitness. Norms may be formulated clearly and openly, but often they remain implicit or adumbrated. Social rules and meanings cannot all be codified in a set of bylaws. On a TV commercial, for example, when a young lady of unabashed nubility saucily peddles hair spray from the locker room of a professional football team, this implies much more about sexual norms than it states about hair spray. Or, as one character pointed out in the opening scene of Henry James' novel, *Portrait of a Lady*: "My dear father, you've lived with the English for thirty years, and you've picked up a good many of the things they say. But you've never learned the things they don't say." Accordingly, not all norms are explicit, nor, considering their nature, should we expect them to be. This is as relevant to aging as it is to other situations. Basically, implicit norms simply inhere in people's expectations about what is appropriate to a role. Consequently, it is often embedded less in explicit norms than in latent assumptions and evaluative standards. Implicit norms remain an endemic problem and a bane of all socialization research.

The explicitness of norms is highly variable, and the extent of that variation may be a function of many factors. For example, one might expect greater explicitness about more central, sacred norms, such as those rather crudely exemplified by the Ten Commandments. But under some circumstances, many moral values are often carefully left unstated. Or one might expect greater explicitness with the norms of a formal position, some of them token or ideal expressions. The more a role approximates a bureaucratic post, the more formalized and overt are its specifications, as in a job description. Similarly, the more a role approximates a profession with technical qualifications, legal responsibilities and authority, the more likely are its formal norms to be embedded in explicit rules and standards. But the norms of most roles are not so overt, and the more remote the role from a formal position, the more likely are the real norms to be implicit.

Aside from these patent factors, norms should also be implicit under several other conditions. First, when they are regarded as virtually **self-evident.** Then they represent common understandings that require no overt formulation; they can be left unstated in the manner of symbols found in art, advertising, or entertainment whose meanings are reasonably clear. Their implicit character reflects a set of shared meanings so commonly understood that they are simply taken for granted without explication. In other words, cognitive and normative areas of genuine consensus are often left implicit.

Second, norms may be implicit when a rather pervasive value takes **many forms** across situations. Then norms should ideally adapt a larger value to a specific context and give substance to it in that setting. But in such situations norms are often left quite implicit. For example, members of a university faculty may share many basic values by virtue of being colleagues (e.g., academic freedom, and respecting research more than teaching or scholarship more than administration). But the criteria of professional creativity and technical competence vary in substance from one department to another. Completely different norms—all subsumed under the rubric, "standards"—are used in the departments of music, physics, English, physiology, architecture, social work, art, psychology, mathematics, drama, and philosophy. Thus, the norms that inform evaluation in any one of these fields may be left rather vague and implicit. By the same token, the criteria for a "significant" contribution to a field might be quite indefinite. The judgment of an individual case might be easily and confidently made, much more so than the explication of standards on which it was presumably based. Similarly, there may be common agreement on the principle that good parenting involves permissiveness with clear limits. But there may be great disagreement on where to draw the line in particular situations. Accordingly, the expression of general values in specific roles often takes the form of implicit norms. Though commonly assumed to be known and not problematic, these are often ambiguous and subject to much disagreement when they are made explicit.

Third, norms are also left implicit when appropriate standards are simply **ambiguous** and there are few guidelines by which to structure and give direction to a role. That is, when expectations are weak, unclear, and indefinite. This may reflect either a normative vacuum or sheer vagueness. Under these circumstances, norms are usually quite implicit.

Certainly for the aged, norms are not explicated because of ambiguous standards—not because they are self-evident or vary in their form across situations. Old and young alike are simply unclear about the proper role for the elderly.

One final detail warrants brief mention. This concerns the relation between people's previous aspirations or desired life styles and their life chances once they are old. For the elderly, established standards are irrevocably undermined by the social losses of aging and by objective pressures to lower their earlier expectations, although there is no normative rationale for this. Yet major pressures develop to affect the standards by which they judge their own benefits or deprivations. However, unlike conventional role conflicts between competing norms that operate simultaneously, they are faced with incompatible standards that change *sequentially*. Their present equities are posed against their past. Accordingly, these shifting standards involve the continuity or discontinuity of norms in status successions. These changing norms denote the latent continuity-discontinuity problem in the transition to old age and in the adult socialization process generally.

SOCIALIZATION CRITERIA

When norms are mainly implicit, a basic conceptual problem is raised: *the specification of socialization criteria.* For role-specific norms harbor the standards by which socialization can be judged and socialization differences distinguished between individuals and groups. Obviously, in research, such criteria must be objectified and operationalized in order to support an analysis, and much more systematic standards than have typically been used will be necessary in the future. This is simply an idea whose time has come.

While the specification of socialization criteria is simple and clear *in principle*, its application to any given role is complicated by numerous factors: by ambiguity and vagueness, by implicit rather than explicit standards, by variability of norms in space and time, by ideal-real discrepancies, by normative alternatives, by loose consensus or even dissensus, and so on.[4]

These difficulties are acute in the definition of norms for older persons. It is terribly complex precisely because the standards of behavior appropriate for them seem quite open and unspecified. Thereby the socialization problem becomes complicated because there seem to be few behavioral pre-

---

4. Irving Rosow, "Professionalization of Social Work Students," Final Report to Social and Rehabilitation Service, Dept. of Health, Education and Welfare, 1969.

scriptions, and the expectations are vague and ambiguous. Hence, the specific goals of socialization are amorphous and the peculiar role content is unclear. Yet the prospective socialization of the elderly is subject to the same theoretical requirements as that of other roles. Insofar as possible, their socialization must also be related to definite norms that are specific to old age. We will examine this in detail momentarily.

This section has explicitly set forth the basic assumptions about social norms on which the present analysis is predicated. Norms can be slippery, changing, almost Protean in concept, congenially adapting to the biases and comfort of the reader. But such transient meanings are poor servants in the development of an argument; they serve only to subvert it, much in the fashion of autistic perception, by destroying the common meanings on which it depends. Therefore, we offer these premises with the explicit caveat that the analysis is based on these principles, not on others.

5. *Norms for Old People*

AGAINST this general background, what are the social norms for the aged? What distinctive standards apply to them? What specific values and behavior are they expected to have simply by virtue of being *old*? Furthermore, how does age modify the norms of their other statuses?

In general, gerontologists have blithely assumed that there is a distinctive role for older people, a specifiable set of belief and action that is expected of the aged. Even though Ernest Burgess early posed the paradox of the roleless role of the elderly,[1] sociologists have all but completely ignored it. And even though revering Burgess' sagacity in other respects, gerontologists have paid little attention to its possible implications. The uncritical assumption seems to be that if there is a status, there must be a significant role. Or given the position of an older person, there must perforce be a corresponding body of substantial responsibilities and prerogatives that shape his or her life.

---

1. Ernest Burgess, "Personal and Social Adjustment in Old Age," in Milton Derber (ed.), *The Aged and Society* (Champaign, Ill.: Industrial Relations Research Association, 1950) 138–56.

But is this necessarily true? Do all social positions have significant expectations and norms? A careful study of the gerontological literature shows that this simply is *not* the case. While there are definite statistical features of the older population, many of which document their declining life chances and role losses, there are few *normative* preferences about an old person's conduct. Rather the standards of appropriate behavior are quite open and flexible, and the norms are limited, weak, and ambiguous. The socialization problem is complicated because there are few behavioral prescriptions and only vague expectations of them. Except for some minor shibboleths, the aged role is basically amorphous and its peculiar content quite unclear. Where earlier age transitions are marked by new responsibilities and expectations, this is not particularly true for the later stages of life. Therefore, the specific goals and possible objectives of socialization are at best vague and attenuated.

THE LITERATURE

Let us now consider the relevant literature. Because many norms may well be implicit, we cannot expect to assemble a list that resembles the formal specifications of a civil service job. But some expectations and standards have been explored and made explicit by scholars. Therefore, among those that are available in research, what do the *normative* ones indicate?

We can start with the massive compendium of research findings of Matilda Riley and Anne Foner and their associates at Rutgers.[2] This is the most authoritative and comprehensive summary of gerontological studies ever undertaken. While it is impossible for even the most ambitious inventory

---

2. Matilda Riley and Anne Foner, *Aging and Society, Volume One: An Inventory of Research Findings* (New York: Russell Sage Foundation, 1968).

to be literally exhaustive, this one is quite definitive and particularly impressive for its thorough coverage. Basically, it cites no work on the general socialization to old age and little more on norms for the elderly. The index contains one solitary entry on **Socialization,** a section of a scant six column inches in a volume of 636 pages. This refers solely to the process of institutionalization of the aged, which is not our present problem. But there is no coverage or research cited on the socialization to old age outside these institutions.

Further, under **Norms,** the index contains only six entries that are scattered among eight pages. These items are extremely ambiguous about *normative* expectations for the aged in our sense of the term. For the most part, the results are of three kinds: (1) purely descriptive statistics on patterns of behavior, such as frequency of intergenerational contact within the family; (2) sheer predictive expectations, such as people's anticipation of loneliness in the event of being widowed; and (3) preferences that *older* persons have, such as the continuation of activity in organizations. While the latter are normative, they focus on the views of old people themselves without reference to the views of other age groups. Finally, there is a small body of genuine social norms that does reflect social definitions among all adults. Essentially these indicate negative attitudes towards institutionalization of the elderly when this is avoidable, a strong endorsement of their living independently as long as possible, and preferred forms of intergenerational reciprocity within the family— such as financial obligations, visiting, mutual aid, etc. The latter emphasize the responsibility of *others* toward the aged, and this is certainly normative in the sense that others have certain obligations to the old. Thereby, it does imply some norms about the rights and prerogatives of the elderly.

However, the overriding significance of these norms is their narrow and limited focus. Basically, they concentrate on several facets of old people's *dependency*. Insofar as dependency problems undeniably increase in later life, this is certainly a legitimate concern, especially as it is an area of potential strain that would involve others. Hence, such definitions do address the problematic. But the range of possible role relationships and the organization of social life transcends issues of dependency alone. In this sense, when norms have such a narrow focus, then clearly they do not represent an extensive sampling of possible relationships, activities, rights, and obligations. And it is in these other, nondependent spheres of life that there is a dearth of expectations to shape roles and provide guidelines. Consequently, aside from dependency needs (about which there is by no means firm consensus), there is a great ambiguity about social norms for the aged.

Elsewhere, in a recent study of 400 young, middle-aged and old adults, Bernice Neugarten and her colleagues report on judgments about behavior that is considered appropriate for people of different ages.[3] They find that in evaluating a person's behavior, sheer age is more important as a criterion to older judges than to younger ones. Also, as they age, people perceive that social norms become more liberal and less constraining, and this in itself is quite significant. But the data do *not* report on specific *norms for older persons*, those behaviors deemed peculiarly appropriate for the aged. The data consisted of thirty-nine items of behavior pertaining to three institutional areas: career, family, and life style. Each item was approved or disapproved for actors of three different ages. These ages varied according to the item, as, for example, a woman wearing a two-piece bathing suit to the beach when she is 18, 30 or 45; or deciding to have another child when she is 30, 37 or 45. Of the six hypothetical cases, the *oldest* actor was 70 in one instance, 55 in

---

3. Bernice Neugarten, Joan Moore and John Lowe, "Age Norms, Age Constraints, and Adult Socialization," *American Journal of Sociology*, 70 (1965) 710–17.

another, and 45 or less in the remaining four. However, there were simply no data reported on behavior approved for older persons, so that norms for the aged were not adduced.

Lipman's research in Florida is one of the most compelling studies attesting to the lack of norms about appropriate sex roles in the household after retirement.[4] He reported that the morale of couples in retirement was related to their development of a consensus about new domestic functions for the husband. He found that the degree of their consensus and the range of their adaptations varied greatly. This variation is a crucial indication that the culture provides them with no definitions or guidelines about the proper activities of a retired husband. The adjustment and role crystallization are completely dependent on the *private* definitions that separate couples develop. Those that worked out a satisfactory adjustment did so on a purely personal basis, while many others, of course, did not find any satisfactory pattern. But neither group, nor any subgroup, could be considered deviant, for in the absence of any normative expectations, all patterns were culturally acceptable.

Elsewhere, Smith did a comprehensive review of ninety-seven studies of the family in old age and summarized the collective results in detail.[5] He abstracted a total of fifty-seven discrete findings in five different categories (relations of husband and wife, older parents and adult children, etc.). These are valuable summaries, but the bulk of them simply describe modal patterns of interaction among various family members. Of the fifty-seven findings, only *three* were essentially *normative* prescriptions of intergenerational obligations. Briefly, the aged and their children "are expected" to

---

4. Aaron Lipman, "Role Conceptions and Morale of Couples in Retirement," *Journal of Gerontology*, 16 (1961) 267–71.

5. Harold Smith, "Family Interaction Patterns of the Aged: A Review," in Arnold Rose and Warren Peterson (eds.), *Older People and their Social World* (Philadelphia: F. A. Davis, 1965) 143–61.

maintain close ties; children "should assume responsibility" for older parents in need; and the independence of the respective conjugal family units "is considered sacrosanct," including the "preferred" maintenance of separate residences.[6] In other words, only a scant 5 percent of the observed patterns could possibly be construed as normative, and these were rather vague. They did not indicate behavior preferred in concrete situations, and the principles for judging this were sketchy. For example, separate residences are quite clear, but close ties are ambiguous. Or in judging the responsibility for older persons in need, whose claims come first when there is a conflict, the grandparents' or the grandchildren's? When resources are limited, as they invariably are, whose claim takes precedence, a grandparent's operation or a grandchild's college tuition, and how should this be determined? When a middle-aged man cannot make a living, should he move to another section of the country where there are jobs, or should he remain where he is because his elderly parents are there? If he decides to move, should his parents move where he does, or should they stay in their home town where their friends are located? If an old widow living alone is losing her eye-sight and does not get along with her daughter-in-law, what should be done? Usually conflicts take the form of such dilemmas, and choices must be made to resolve them. What then are the norms for older people's expectations? How do values about the aged guide the decisions that are made? What should an old person expect as right and proper? The three norms abstracted by Smith provide only the vaguest guidelines for structuring older people's reciprocal expectations in the family, both within and between generations, specifically on age grounds.

Further, as the study of Neugarten and her associates indicated, norms become more flexible and liberal with ad-

6. *Ibid.*, pp. 152–54.

vancing age and allow people a progressively greater range of personal choice in ordering their lives. This is most apparent in the early research of Havighurst and Albrecht which probably still contains more relevant data than any other single study on social norms for the aged.[7] Although it suffers from various sampling and other methodological defects, the appendices contain valuable materials on a broad range of role activities for older men and women.

These warrant a more intensive secondary analysis than we can present, but we can review the data in a general way. In 1949 and 1951 Havighurst and Albrecht drew samples of Prairie City, a small midwestern town. They submitted examples of older people's hypothetical behavior for the respondents to approve or disapprove. The conduct of men and women was judged separately. There was a combined total of 128 behavioral items classified into six institutional spheres (political and civic affairs, church, family, work and finances, clubs and organizations, recreation and leisure). Simple public approval scores were developed for each item, and these represented the data on norms. Note that *they were genuine social norms* in our terms. This part of the interview was complemented by interviews with a special sample of one hundred older persons in order to rate their activity in thirteen specific roles within the six institutional spheres.

The evaluations of old people's hypothetical activities show several results. First, many of the attitudes are *not* age-specific, but reflect basic norms for *all* adult townspeople, not simply the aged. Many of these are tightly bound up with the Puritan ethic of rural America and the strong social controls of conservative village life. The strongest values delineate their ideal conception of the good life. The sharpest approval and disapproval are reserved for such

7. Robert Havighurst and Ruth Albrecht, *Older People* (New York: Longmans and Green, 1953).

Puritanical virtues as hard work, thrift, independence, and religiosity, and for contacts with relatives and friends in an active social life, especially in public activities of the church and other formal organizations. The most approved (prescribed) activities include voting regularly; keeping in regular touch with friends and relatives by visit, phone, or mail; spending "most" of one's time on an active special interest or hobby; being very actively involved with the church, attending services regularly, reading the Bible daily, and drawing a great deal of comfort from religion; and pursuing an active social life in the community together with one's spouse, especially among persons one's own age. Basically, these are activities approved for people of all ages, not just the old.

The age-specific prescriptions are considerably fewer and focus on income maintenance, the family, and the church. Older persons should presumably become even more interested in religion and the church than they previously were; they should be greatly interested in their grandchildren and great-grandchildren; they should maintain ritual contact with their children at definite times, especially holidays, and occasionally look after grandchildren when the parents are away; but otherwise they should lead a life separate from their children; and they should maintain financial independence as long as possible, primarily through work, or if retired, through management of property and investments. Old-age pensions are acceptable only after savings are exhausted. Such independence themes are, of course, quite general and are only formulated here in terms of old age.

The strongly disapproved (proscribed) norms follow similar patterns and also focus on general rather than age-specific standards. Many are simply the obverse of ideally approved activities. For example, "Visits friends and receives visits in his own home" is strongly approved, while its converse, "No longer entertains groups of friends at home," is strongly disapproved. Furthermore, many of the proscrip-

tions that seem age-specific are essentially artifactual, for
they simply extend certain basic values into old age by qualifying the item wording. Thus, nominally different items are
actually equivalent, even though one has an age qualification
added. For example, "Does not belong to clubs and is not
interested in them" (general) is basically the same as, "Has
dropped out of all clubs as he has grown older." The involvement in local club life is so strongly valued that its rejection
is virtually intolerable. This value is so pervasive that it completely vitiates the qualification about aging. Consequently,
the responses are essentially general rather than age-specific
proscriptions. Except for some familial relationships, this
"halo effect" covers many other presumably age-specific proscriptions.

Against this background, the sharpest proscriptions
condemn a life of inactivity and solitude: not belonging to
or dropping out of clubs; losing touch with and seeing very
little of friends; no longer entertaining at home or attending
social affairs with spouse; living quietly without social contacts; never taking out-of-town trips; or just sitting around
doing nothing. Also strongly condemned are a disinterest in
politics and having nothing to do with the church. Even
more strongly disapproved are weak or broken family ties
(disinterest in children or grandchildren; not keeping in
touch with relatives) or insufficient independence of adult
children (living with and arguing with them; depending on
them to decide where one lives; depriving oneself to conserve
an inheritance for them). Violation of the Puritan ethic also
comes in for strong censure (taking no responsibility for
managing the home; going on relief though still able to work
and earn something; using pension or relief money for luxuries or extravagances). These are obviously ideal norms.

But the most interesting proscriptions are violations of
sacred values. They represent extremes of disapproved behavior, including: getting a divorce, spending a lot of time

in a tavern with old friends, becoming a scoffer at formal religion, making speculative investments in property and stocks, and getting married to someone thirty years younger. To be sure, marrying someone thirty years one's junior or using relief money for extravagant luxuries are extremely unusual and possibly gauche. But all hints of self-indulgence, iconoclasm, and financial imprudence were regarded as immoral and strictly taboo in the Protestant heartland of 1950.

Beyond the foregoing matters lay the sphere of tolerance and low moral compulsion, and one is impressed by its scope. This encompassed the intermediate behavior that was fully acceptable. If not prescribed or preferred, at least certainly *permitted*. This offered definite latitude for moderate conformity, for behavior that was neither ideal nor extreme, but did not violate acceptable limits. So long as deviance did not openly flout local norms and proscriptions, even Prairie City could tolerate considerable variation in older people's roles and activity. So long as a person was not a virtual recluse, but occasionally made a token social appearance, this was probably tolerable. If he made even minor obeisance to family solidarity and the church, this was also probably acceptable. In other words, the central issue was not simply the level of a person's social activity, but his nominal acceptance of the *legitimacy* of the local values. If he were occasionally willing to make symbolic gestures of compliance and did not militantly make contemptuous waves, this was probably all that was necessary. Thus, in all likelihood, the norms of Prairie City allowed enough scope for a limited conformity that did not openly challenge local standards.

The crucial theoretical point, however, is that, except for some family relationships, the norms in Prairie City were neither *age-specific* nor particularly *real*. The concern with sacred elements of the culture simply affirmed general standards of ideal behavior for all adults. Townspeople of all ages were expected to value family ties, public participation in community activities, a strong religious life, economic independence, and similar virtues of a vigorous Protestant ethic—probably tempered by some flexibility. In contrast to the actual behavior on most items, *extreme* observance of these ideals was probably rare and sporadic. Certainly we have no significant data on ideal-real discrepancies in Prairie City or on the social price of nonconformity. We cannot analyze ideal-real differences from the role activity inventory of the special subsample, for this is not comparable to the behavioral items in the study of norms. Such an analysis would require the same set of categories for any meaningful comparison.

Many of these materials from a midwestern village of that period are probably not only atypical of America in the 'seventies, but certainly of the nation as a whole at the time of the original study. If the same research had been carried out in 1950 on a national probability sample, not to mention a metropolitan sample, the results might have been drastically different and shown more flexible expectations about the aged. Even the ideal norms would certainly have been less rigid, less preoccupied with the church and all forms of public activity—with highly visible behavior subject to constant scrutiny and control. Thus, the social pressures would probably have been easier and less arbitrary. Certainly in urban and metropolitan centers, the norms and expectations for older people would be much looser. We would expect them to be less intense and less extreme, with less investment in sacred community values, with fewer requirements and prohibitions, and a broad, flexible range of acceptable behavior. In other words, urban values are generally more permissive than rural.

But note that the significant terms of discourse do not concern age norms per se so much as rural-urban differences in social pressures, conformity, and social control. Prairie City offers a picture of small-town values of the period, not a portrayal of the distinctive position of its older citizens and the special norms that apply to them.

As people age, their responsibilities and power decline sharply, limiting the social consequences of their action and their ability to affect others adversely. Therefore, there is little social stake in their behavior and correspondingly small concern with the options open to them and the choices they actually make. For they have little effect on other people. To be sure, the objective limitations of their declining health and income may restrict their social participation. But *within these limitations*, more alternatives are available to them—specifically as role options—in shaping their private lives than ever before. So long as they do not become bizarre and do not present special burdens to others, then within their means they can do very largely as they want and may live as they wish. Their roles are essentially free, open to more personal preference and choice in fashioning their lives than at any previous life stage. While old people tend to be excluded by members of younger generations, the norms for them are few, mild and flexible, neither onerous nor restrictive. *The very real constraints on them are objective, not normative.*

There should, however, be a qualifying caveat. We are not categorically asserting that there are literally *no* norms for older persons, for some do operate. But for the most part, these focus on intergenerational family ties. For example, Townsend's research on the aged in British working class families has shown the distinctive function of the grandmother who is expected to hold together a viable quasimatriarchal network of her adult daughters and their children.[8] So long as she is competent and not senile, her authority is relatively unquestioned. And she is responsible for keeping the group

---

8. Peter Townsend, *Family Life of Old People* (London: Routledge & Kegan Paul, 1957).

cohesive, adjudicating differences, counseling on various personal problems, assisting with child care, directing ritual occasions, and generally functioning as group leader and mentor in the lives of her daughters and their children, as befits a proper "earth mother." When the grandmother dies or becomes senile or her health fails so that she can no longer discharge these functions, the group typically falls apart. Sisters may continue to see each other individually, but their institutional linkages are disrupted and finished. Each is on her way in middle age to the establishment of her own matriarchal lineage with her own female progeny. The responsible role of the British working-class grandmother is most unusual for its clarity and significant social functions.

Further, my own research has established older people's preferred sources of help for various needs when their family situations differ.[9] For example, local children are the primary source of care for immobilizing illness, but when children are not available there is a range of acceptable substitutes, including relatives, neighbors, and other friends. But this flexibility does *not* apply to sources of financial aid, which are limited to adult children (or for the childless, to local relatives), or to various formal organizations. Neighbors and friends are unconditionally excluded for financial assistance, nonlocal relatives are virtually ineligible, and requests to nonlocal children are drastically reduced. Yet, while there is little hard evidence on this, similar standards apparently apply throughout adult life. This would indicate that while there are definite norms about reciprocity and help, these are not peculiar to old age.

Other research has consistently documented the significant contraction of the social world of the elderly. This is most conspicuous in their lower participation outside the

---

9. Irving Rosow, *Social Integration of the Aged* (New York: Free Press, 1967), Chapter 5.

family rather than within it. Activity in formal organizations and contact with friends are sharply reduced, but there is no corresponding attrition of interaction within the family. This is particularly true for old people who are nominally "disengaged."[10] Though these patterns are statistically established, their normative status is most equivocal. The maintenance of family ties is, of course, clearly normative. But the reduction of nonfamilial associations is not necessarily preferred, nor is there any evidence that it is strongly valued. It is simply a fact that indicates one possible choice in the range of acceptable options open to older persons. Indeed, there is not even a strong correlation between intragenerational family norms as these are reflected in various patterns of behavior.[11]

These findings epitomize much more extensive results in the literature. They simply illustrate the basic point that such norms as exist for older persons refer overwhelmingly to reciprocal relationships within the family. To this extent they are limited, confined to a major but single institutional sphere. They do provide some general guidance on intergenerational association in the family, but other areas of life are virtually ignored. Even though old people are admonished by well-meaning advisors to "be active," there are almost no norms that specify and give meaning to this admonition,

---

10. Grace Chellam, "Disengagement Theory: Awareness of Death and Self-Engagement" (Unpublished D.S.W. Thesis, Case Western Reserve University, 1964); Elaine Cumming and William Henry, *Growing Old* (New York: Basic Books, 1961).

11. Alan Kerckhoff, "Husband-Wife Expectations and Reactions to Retirement," in Ida Simpson and John McKinney (eds.), *Social Aspects of Aging* (Durham: Duke University Press, 1966) 160–72; "Norm-Value Clusters and the 'Strain Toward Consistency' Among Older Married Couples," in *ibid.*, 138–59, and "Nuclear and Extended Family Relationships," in Ethel Shanas and Gordon Streib (eds.), *Social Structure and the Family: Generational Relations* (Englewood Cliffs, N.J.: Prentice-Hall, 1965) 93–112. Also cf. Gordon Streib, "Family Patterns in Retirement," *Journal of Social Issues*, 14, No. 2 (1958) 46–60.

that provide even guides (much less prescriptions) for sheer role *content* and activity—in a word, what older people should do with their available time and energy and how they should shape their lives.

Briefly then, the norms provide almost no expectations that effectively *structure* an older person's activities and general pattern of life. His adjustment in this respect results essentially from his individual decisions and choices, from *personal* definitions of what is appropriate and desirable. There are no significant expectations and roles for him. In this sense, an old person's life is basically "roleless," unstructured by the society, and conspicuously lacking in norms, especially for nonfamilial relationships.

This contrasts sharply with earlier life stages. At various crucial points, a limited number of key decisions about education, marriage, family, career, and the good life are extremely consequential for shaping life styles and sheer role content. The goals and implications of these key decisions introduce refined structure to people's lives, not only of specific roles, but often of daily time budgets. Consequently, role requirements do shape larger life patterns in earlier life stages, but not in old age. Given certain decisions in youth and middle age, the norms limit further options but impose no comparable restrictions in old age. Within the realistic limitations of health and income, there are few norms that structure older people's roles. Again, the constraints on them are objective, not normative.

The amorphous norms place the elderly in a further predicament, one that is aggravated when they have a significant loss of major roles. When they are socially defined as old, this subtly shifts them from an achieved to an ascribed status position.[12] Sarbin has analyzed the consequences of

---

12. Irving Rosow, "The Social Context of the Aging Self," *Gerontologist*, 13 (Spring, 1973) 82–87.

conformity and deviance in ascribed and achieved roles.[13] Briefly, he argues that in achieved roles, conformity and performance are rewarded, but failure is seldom penalized. On the other hand, in ascribed roles, conformity is not particularly rewarded, but failure is punished. The anomaly for the aged is that with amorphous norms, there are few criteria for judging either conformity or deviance, their success or failure. Hence, there is little basis for any system of reward and punishment, even among the militant aged.[14] This is a genuine discontinuity in life that weakens incentives for becoming old. It also emphasizes the fact that old people's attitudes and behavior have little social consequence and that society has little stake in them. Yet the clarity of roles and a system of rewards geared to conformity are equally relevant to the social motives of all age groups.[15] Therefore, when norms

13. Theodore Sarbin, "Notes on the Transformation of Social Identity," in L. M. Roberts, N. S. Greenfield and M. H. Miller (eds.), *Comprehensive Mental Health* (Madison: University of Wisconsin Press, 1968) 97–115.

14. Low interdependence and competition among the aged even preclude the theoretical possibility of introducing differential rewards as a means of stimulating individual or group performance. Cf. L. Keith Miller and Robert Hamblin, "Interdependence, Differential Rewarding and Productivity," *American Sociological Review*, 28 (1963) 768–78.

15. Richard Filer and Desmond O'Connell, "Motivation of Aging Persons," *Journal of Gerontology*, 19 (1964) 15–22; Leonard Goodstein, "Personal Adjustment Factors and Retirement," *Geriatrics*, 17 (1962) 41–45; Woodrow Hunter and Helen Maurice, *Older People Tell Their Story* (Ann Arbor: University of Michigan, Division of Gerontology, 1953); Edward Ludwig and Robert Eichhorn, "Age and Disillusionment: A Study of Value Changes Associated with Aging," *Journal of Gerontology*, 22 (1967) 59–65. To be sure, some have argued that flexible norms may be as effective as those which are absolute in securing performance *after* socialization has taken place (Snell Putney and Russell Middleton, "Ethical Relativism and Anomia," *American Journal of Sociology*, 67 [1962] 430–38). However, the amorphousness of norms is another matter entirely, particularly in the process of socialization itself. See the contrasts delineated in Howard Becker and James Carper, "The Development of Identification with an Occupation," *American Journal of Sociology*, 61 (1956) 289–98, and "The Elements of Identification with an Occupation," *American Sociological Review*, 21 (1956) 341–48. Moreover, the general function of rewards in motivating performance is reasonably clear (Melvin

are vague and there are no significant incentives, there is no foundation for viable social motives among the aged. The fact that norms for the elderly are so amorphous is absolutely basic to the prospect of their socialization to old age.

But let us momentarily make a different assumption: that current research is inadequate and that there are significant age-specific norms that have simply not been identified. If this were true, it would still not foreclose the issue. For even if viable norms were established, this would not necessarily assure effective socialization to them. Clear role prescriptions per se provide no guarantee of successful socialization to the role. That would present an empirical as well as theoretical issue. Therefore, the sheer presence of norms is a *necessary, but not sufficient* condition of effective socialization. While there can be little socialization without norms, the converse does not inevitably follow—that the existence of norms assures effective socialization.

SUBCULTURE AND GROUP CONSCIOUSNESS OF THE AGED

One related problem warrants attention, namely, the assertion that conditions for the crystallization of norms for older people are actually growing. The foremost exponent of this position is the late Arnold Rose, who enunciated this view in a pair of companion articles. In the first paper, he argues that the conditions favoring a subculture of the aging include the growing number of old people, their generally superior health, the common problems they face, and various trends tending to segregate them, whether voluntarily or involuntarily, as in forced retirement.[16] He concludes from

Tumin, "Rewards and Task-Orientations," *American Sociological Review*, 20 [1955] 419–23).

16. Arnold Rose, "The Subculture of the Aging," in Arnold Rose and Warren Peterson (eds.), *Older People and their Social World* (Philadelphia: F. A. Davis, 1965) 3–16.

this that a group consciousness is emerging among the aged, although admittedly among only a *minority* of them. The major mechanisms of this identification are presumably special organizations for older people, such as Golden Age clubs of various kinds. These attract the elderly, allow them to discuss their common problems, and consequently generate pressures for social action. At the same time, their group consciousness militates against the negative self-conceptions of the aged and generates resentment at the discrimination against older persons. Identification with the group fosters a *desire to associate with age peers*, rather than with younger people, as an expression of *group pride*. "With this group pride has come self-acceptance as a member of an esteemed group."[17]

In his second paper, Rose compares groups of old people who do and do not have this positive group consciousness in order to clarify the kind of persons who are in the vanguard of this putative development.[18] In general, he finds that the aging-Conscious are more active than the non-aging-Conscious in formal organizations, both religious and secular, age-graded and non-age-graded. Their leisure time is also more active, and they interact more frequently with relatives, friends, and neighbors. Furthermore, they are politically more involved and militant. Yet, despite their far higher levels of interaction and participation, significantly more of the aging-Conscious want to have still more social activity.

Rose raises a major theoretical problem, but poses it in terms that seriously weaken his analysis. First, he simply assumes that the growth of conditions favorable to group consciousness necessarily produces such identification. But, obviously, this is not inevitable. For example, the objective

---

17. *Ibid.*, p. 14.
18. Arnold Rose, "Group Consciousness among the Aging," in Arnold Rose and Warren Peterson (eds.), *Older People and their Social World*, pp. 19–36.

self-interest of white-collar workers would probably be most rationally served through their strong unionization. Yet status considerations have militated against their development of a working class consciousness and ideology. Consequently, white-collar workers have been notoriously slower than manual workers in forming and joining unions to protect themselves through collective bargaining. Further, Rose has ignored the powerful forces that militate against older people's identification with the aged when they must place themselves publicly in an invidious position. This problem has been examined elsewhere in detail.[19] The weakness of Rose's case is that people do not always pursue their self-interest rationally; objective interests may be sacrificed to status considerations; and consequently, propitious conditions do not necessarily produce the rational action he envisions.

Accordingly, the eventual emergence of group consciousness among the aged is at best extremely problematic. Rose acknowledges that only a minority of older persons now has such an identification, but he asserts that there is a definite trend in its development. At the same time, he offers no evidence of such a trend; this remains an empirical issue that time will resolve, but one whose results cannot be assumed as a foregone conclusion. What is at stake here is the crucial conversion of older people from a social *category* into viable, self-conscious *groups*, functioning as corporate entities, with group supports, definite standards, and distinctive life styles that they consciously share. Under such optimal conditions, norms and roles for older persons might possibly develop, but this cannot be taken for granted. We will analyze this further in the last section of the book.

Against this background, another critical issue is whether Rose's aging-Conscious persons are typical or atypical

---

19. Irving Rosow, *Social Integration of the Aged*, esp. Chapter I. Also, cf. Nancy Anderson, "The Significance of Age Categories for Older Persons," *Gerontologist*, 7 (1967) 164–67.

of the aged. Are they the forerunners of a general trend, *leaders* who personify emergent tendencies of the old, or are they actually nonleadership *deviants*? Rose obviously regards them as leaders of social change. But in many respects they suggest a sample of elderly deviants, people who are atypical of the age group and lacking in significant leadership potential as agents of change. In this sense, they strongly resemble one social type found in my own research, the Insatiables, who were marked by a frenetic pattern of hyperactivity that served as a defense against the anxieties and losses of old age.[20] Despite very high levels of interaction and association, they wanted still more friends and social activity. Yet there was no evidence that they were unusually popular or respected, that they exemplified leaders who crystallized inchoate, amorphous frustrations and channeled these into group solidarity. That Rose's aging-Conscious were activists is clear. That they resented the losses of old age is also clear from his data. He correctly points out that as previous occupations, roles, and power "fade into the past, they are of diminishing influence in conferring prestige . . . . Because most of the changes associated with the assumption of the role and self-conception of being elderly are negatively evaluated in American culture . . . there is no compensatory attribution of prestige."[21] As one old woman in another study put it, "I am holding on to life with both hands, but I feel that as life goes on society pries loose one finger after another."[22]

In general, the potential leadership of the aging-Con-

---

20. Irving Rosow, *Social Integration of the Aged*, pp. 113–18.

21. Arnold Rose, "The Subculture of the Aging." For a systematic analysis of the theoretical ground for status attrition in old age, see Irving Rosow, "Retirement Leisure and Social Status," in Duke University Council on Aging and Human Development, *Proceedings of Seminars, 1965–1969* (Durham, N.C.: Duke University Center for the Study of Aging and Human Development, 1969) 249–57.

22. Mark Zborowski, "Aging and Recreation," *Journal of Gerontology*, 17 (1962) 302–09.

scious seems to be extremely tenuous. They appear to be a small group of older *militants* protesting against the losses of age and their inevitable marginality and obsolescence in the larger society. To this extent, affiliation with the aged is comprehensible as a defensive reaction, which slows the corrosive effects of time on their social position and selects a sheltered arena of social action. While this might be a reasonable response to the shrinking opportunities elsewhere, it is a far cry from a full-blooded identification with the age group. To be sure, two-thirds of them think that as they have grown older they have more in common with their peers, that there should be more organizations for older people, and that the aged should organize to demand their rights—even though only 19 percent believe that the old are treated badly by younger persons and 31 percent that they are prevented from doing things because younger people run everything.[23]

Yet another glaring inconsistency appears in Rose's data. In his analysis, identification with the aged creates the desire to associate with peers *to the exclusion* of younger persons. However, in his sample the preference to associate with peers marked 43 percent of the non-aging-Conscious, but only 15 percent of the aging-Conscious.[24] Further, 82 percent of the aging-Conscious claim that their companion's age makes no difference or that they prefer younger people. Such data expose serious discrepancies that Rose ignores. When only one in seven actually prefer the company of their peers, this is a sharp denial of group pride—it is not a rejection of the young and an identification with the old. Rather, these inconsistencies indicate defensive reactions among the aging, even among the more militant aging-Conscious minority. In other words, if vigorous older people want to be highly involved with others but cannot be meaningfully affiliated with the middle aged, then their main recourse is to associate with

23. Arnold Rose, "Group Consciousness among the Aging."
24. *Ibid.*

their peers. This is scarcely positive identification; it simply makes a virtue of necessity. It is in sharp contrast to the fierce loyalties and group solidarity of adolescents. It is also fundamentally different from the positive identification that would stimulate the growth of group consciousness among the aged in general. Hence, we cannot simply accept Rose's evidence as a definite harbinger of hardening solidarity and the inevitable development of clear norms and role definitions for the elderly.

But aside from the possibility of growing identification in the future, the *conditions* favoring group consciousness are theoretically important, even though they may apply to only a minority of the aged. Rose's position is relevant to this issue, even if not as a basis of prediction, and it will be considered in our subsequent analysis of the possible functions of the peer group for its members.

In summary, just as there are few significant norms for the old, there is no compelling evidence of a waxing group consciousness that would develop new standards. It is very clear that most older people emphatically do *not* identify themselves with the aged and that they are most reluctant to do so. While they may associate with each other privately, they strongly dissociate themselves from their peers publicly.[25]

STRUCTURAL EVIDENCE

To this point, we have established that there is little evidence of a thriving subculture of the aged and presumably only weak, vague norms for them. But as clear as this seems, it is not definitive. We cannot foreclose the issue of amorphous norms at this point because the picture they present may be deceptive and specious.

---

25. For a review of the literature, see Irving Rosow, *Social Integration of the Aged*, Chapter 7, "Identification with the Aged: Peers as Reference Group."

While the normative vacuum may indeed be real, several other possibilities must be taken into account. First, the lack of evidence may result from sheer **inattention.** If we have studied the problem so little, the paucity of data should not be surprising; we may actually be contending with a dearth of research rather than with a poverty of norms. Second, norms may be inadequately **sampled.** Those that have been examined come from a narrow segment of the possible range. Basically, they focus on problems of dependency and intra-familial relationships. Other areas have been largely ignored. This produces an extremely limited picture if only because of what we have left out. Therefore, our skimpy evidence may actually reflect less a scarcity of norms than a defect in sampling them. Finally, if most norms are implicit, then we may be facing **methodological** limitations.[26] Because of conceptual fuzziness or inadequate techniques, implicit norms may simply be eluding our research, somewhat like the crafty old trout who survives in the stream, mocking the clumsy fishermen. Our casual and oblivious assumptions may have diverted our attention from possible latent norms so that we have not sought them out. Or our research designs and tactics may have been too inadvertent and crude to find them.

If any of these alternatives is true, then our assertion of weak norms may be false.[27] In other words, our conclusion may be denying an actual condition. However, *I do not believe this*, and I regard the normative vacuum as *real*. But the possibility of error is not trivial and must be taken seriously. Therefore, we cannot let it rest here; we must pursue it fur-

26. Cf. Irving Rosow, "Professionalization of Social Work Students," Final Report to Social and Rehabilitation Service, Dept. of Health, Education and Welfare, 1969.

27. Clearly, we are dealing here with the epistemological difficulty of *proving* the absence of hypothetical phenomena. There is no logical problem when research demonstrates their presence. But the definitive establishment of their absence tends to be an inconclusive pursuit, one more amenable to consensual than objective resolution.

ther and try to determine whether the vacuum is spurious or genuine.

Perhaps the best approach to this problem is through the principle of structural consistency. It rests on the assumption that *equivalent situations have similar means-ends relationships*. This is the essence of the argument: (1) The typical socialization situation is a means of inculcating given norms as ends. Therefore, (2) if aging resembles such situations in *structure* and *process* (means), then (3) it should also be directed to a target set of norms (ends). But, (4) if there is *no* significant similarity in the structure of the situations, then (5) there is no basis of assuming a coherent body of norms for the aged. These propositions are reduced to the following summary, with the notations representing: (A) Aging, (N) Norms, and (S) Socializing Structures.

(1) $S \rightarrow N_1$
(2) If $A = S$
(3) $\therefore A \rightarrow N_2$
(4) If $A \neq S$
(5) $\therefore A \nrightarrow N_2$

If socialization represents a purposive effort to inculcate norms, then logic requires a comparison between the situation of aging and typical socialization situations *with* norms. This would allow one to see how aging fits into the general structure of socialization and whether the usual socialization variables are also operative. For if the aged conform in these respects—if they are subject to the same factors in an analytically similar structure—then the normative vacuum would become suspect. We would assume that comparable elements and processes should lead to parallel results; an apparent weakness of age norms would then seem specious, and we should return to the drawing board to reanalyze the shortcomings of the evidence. But if there is *little* correspondence between the two situations—if the aged deviate significantly from the effective forces in general socialization models—then the normative vacuum would be quite credible. We would reasonably assume that different structures would not necessarily have similar results. Therefore, if the socializing factors were neligible or absent, then the limitation of norms would be quite tenable. And we could accept our evidence on weak norms as basically valid.[28] At the same time, these results would further demonstrate that the effective socializing forces on aging persons are also weak.

Accordingly, most of the remaining discussion has two primary functions: (1) to provide this consistency check on our estimate of the state of aging norms, and (2) to analyze aging in the general framework of socialization theory, with particular attention to the structure of socialization situations and the major socializing variables. This will serve to clarify the prospects and problems of the socialization to old age within our present institutional arrangements.

---

28. There is a third logical possibility: that there are viable norms to which the aged are not effectively socialized. But this is rather unlikely. If the socializing forces were powerful, the elderly would require strong group supports to counter them, much in the fashion of successful resistance to brain-washing in the Korean War (for citations to the literature, see Irving Rosow, "The Social Context of the Aging Self"). And the aged do not have such effective group supports. If the norms and socializing forces were mild, they would be too inconsequential to represent a significant third alternative.

6. *Properties of Socialization Situations*

JUST AS the gerontological literature has not taken up the problem of socialization, so has the socialization literature virtually ignored old age and given it only cursory attention. For example, in their book on adult socialization, Brim and Wheeler simply mention it once in passing, noting only that certain attitude changes in middle age may be necessary for socialization to old age.[1] In the volume edited by Clausen, the sole notice taken specifically of the aged is Brim's observation that physical decline reduces people's performance and others' expectations of them in the later years.[2] Inkeles goes somewhat further.[3] He sets the task of older persons in familiar terms: learning to give up previous

---

1. Orville Brim and Stanton Wheeler, *Socialization After Childhood* (New York: John Wiley, 1966) 22.
2. Orville Brim, "Adult Socialization," in John Clausen (ed.), *Socialization and Society* (Boston: Little, Brown, 1968) 186–226.
3. Alex Inkeles, "Social Structure and Socialization," in David Goslin (ed.), *Handbook of Socialization Theory and Research* (Chicago: Rand McNally, 1969) 615–32.

statuses and their perquisites.[4] He defines the objective of socializers as that of inducing the elderly to accept their new status (and presumably its limitations), perhaps with the acquisition of new skills such as those appropriate to full-time leisure. These are apparently sound inferences, but of a kind that we have found problematic. Certainly it would be simpler for younger generations if the old were to relinquish previous roles and claims, accepting a new leisure without murmur and graciously fading from the social landscape. Yet on a *societal* level, the young and middle aged might be quite indifferent to anything but the punctual retirement or claims of dependency of the old. While they might consider the decrements and problems of the elderly as unfortunate, they might also view this with detachment as another of life's vicissitudes that does not vitally concern them. In other words, Inkeles' assumptions about expectations are precisely what must be validated. If they should be verified, then it must be shown how these norms are specified and implemented in socialization, how conformity is secured by meaningful incentives, whether of social rewards, duress, or some other means.

Riley and her associates devote more attention to the problem.[5] They adapt Brim and Wheeler's thinking about the individual-societal relationship in which society sets expectations and provides facilities and sanctions for learning a new role, and this is balanced by the person's motives and capacity to learn, his performance, and his conformity or deviance in response to social pressures. On the basis of existing research, they find that older persons have limited capacity and motives for being socialized. While they deal with

---

4. Cf. Harry Bredemeier and Richard Stephenson, *The Analysis of Social Systems* (New York: Holt, Rinehart & Winston, 1962) Chapter 4.

5. Matilda Riley, Anne Foner, Beth Hess and Marcia Toby, "Socialization for the Middle and Later Years," in David Goslin (ed.), *op. cit.*, 951–82.

various organic and social disadvantages, including the loss of social esteem, they pay insufficient attention both to the invidious status the aged are asked to accept and to its effects.[6] Yet they do clearly note the limited societal stake in the socialization to old age, though not linking it directly, as I think it must be, to the dwindling *social responsibility* of the elderly.[7]

> To the extent that some new roles fail to present goals that are valued by society, there can be no clear expectations of constructive performance, facilities and resources for training are likely to be in short supply, and rewards tend to become minimal or even negative. Under these conditions, the individual is given little incentive to learn, and social inputs appear to fall far short of the model of optimum socialization. (963)

The serious reservation about the clarity of norms and the collective investment in socialization to old age calls into question the assumptions of Inkeles that seem so moot. Riley *et al.* find few social pressures that consistently bend the elderly to others' expectations. This brings them to the basic point that is so fundamental throughout my analysis: the lack of socialization criteria.

> Thus, there are no clear and widely shared expectations as to what role occupants will do. . . . Such goallessness is bound up, of course, with the ineffectiveness of sanctions in facilitating socialization. Without clarity in the norms, *specific performances cannot be defined as either conformist or deviant*; nor can appropriate rewards or punishment be meted out. . . . There are few clear expectations and few positive incentives. (964–65; italics inserted)

Yet, despite their clarity, Riley *et al.* sometimes become inconsistent, almost as if the human implications of their

---

6. Irving Rosow, "The Social Context of the Aging Self," *Gerontologist*, 13 (Spring, 1973) 82–87.
7. *Ibid.*

analysis become too implacable and they must search for some relief. For example, in relation to bereavement in widowhood, they say: "The *sanctions* are structured to reward return to normal functioning," yet they presently conclude, "Sanctions for performance in the widow role per se seem largely confined to the indifference accorded to solitary aged individuals. . . . While negative pressures foster withdrawal from the previous role, there are few positive incentives for involvement in the new one." (968–69) Where, then, do the rewards lie for a return to normalcy?

In treating individual adaptations to these various dilemmas, Riley and her colleagues set them in the context of the continuity-discontinuity of roles that we considered earlier at some length. They apply Parsons and Shils' model of possible responses to the discontinuity of norms in role change.[8] Presumably the alternatives open to a person are: (1) to restructure the situation and generate a consistent role; (2) to reduce dissonance by redefining either the old or new role so as to make the aging situation more tolerable; or (3) to lapse into deviance, including withdrawal. In assessing these options, clearly the first alternative is virtually precluded by objective circumstances. The second poses the Orwellian dilemma of renouncing a meaningful past or embracing an unrewarding present. The third may offer the most viable prospect of preserving psychological integrity and a sense of personal worth.

Finally, Riley and her associates consider possible alternatives for the elderly. These presuppose major institutional changes that would create new roles for them. But they do not examine the cumulative effects of a system that would routinely continue to exclude the aged. And to assume the

---

8. Talcott Parsons and Edward Shils, "Values, Motives and Systems of Action," in Talcott Parsons and Edward Shils (eds.), *Toward a General Theory of Action* (Cambridge: Harvard University Press, 1951) 3–29.

basic social changes necessary for new roles may actually be to invoke a *deus ex machina.*

The general perspective of Riley and her colleagues is certainly congenial to my own, for they touch briefly on several factors that are necessarily central to all but the most superficial or pollyanna view of socialization to old age. Obviously they recognize some of the inherent dilemmas of the problem. At the same time, they have difficulty in accepting the unavoidable implications of their own analysis. This is evident in the inconsistency mentioned above. While they steadfastly assert that there are no effective social norms in aging and, therefore, no criteria for conformity, they nonetheless proceed to discuss socialization as if there were, particularly in the context of retirement and widowhood. After all, the sheer acquiescence in a fact of life does not necessarily signify socialization.[9] This anomaly in the article understandably leaves their discussion fuzzy at points, in contrast to their incisiveness about vague norms. To assert that the necessary conditions are absent and then to proceed as if they were present simply vitiates the very concept of socialization.

Further, their treatment is somewhat weakened by what may be termed a lack of weighting. In filling the various categories of a conceptual model, they handle the elements as if these were of equal weight or significance. For example, we can note the possible resources for socialization of the aged, but these are often ineffective in the face of their strong resistance. Golden Age clubs may be viewed technically as a facility, but they have reached only a smattering of the elderly because of their disinterest and fear of stigmatizing themselves publicly.[10] Similarly, there is a disproportionate em-

---

9. Dennis Wrong, "The Oversocialized Conception of Man," *American Sociological Review*, 26 (1961) 183–93.

10. Irving Rosow, *Social Integration of the Aged* (New York: Free Press, 1967).

phasis on committed socializing agents and the investment in socializing activity. Again, there is an inconsistency between the discussion and conclusions. Adherence to a conceptual framework does not always keep the model's elements in perspective. A mere classification of factors is not an assessment of their relative strength or importance. The issue of weighting is more a matter of balance than of substance, but it serves to adumbrate the issues rather than clarify them.

One final point. The analysis by Riley and her colleagues differs from my own in emphasis, essentially in the issues we address. They deal with socialization in global terms, but aging in more prosaic detail. I reverse this, considering old age globally, but socialization in much greater detail. Where they examine little in the socialization situation itself, I concentrate on this. My emphasis is on the structure of the socialization situation, the conditions that affect it, and the factors that govern its processes. Thus, my focus on the socialization field serves to complement their concerns.

NB

NECESSARY CONDITIONS OF SOCIALIZATION *cannot able*

While many factors may be conducive to socialization, Brim and Wheeler have suggested three basic conditions that are necessary to its success.[11] First, the actor must have **knowledge** of what is expected of him in terms of the norms of his new position. He may acquire this over a period of time, as in most formal training situations, or he may learn it quickly. But he must have a cognitive map of the content, activities, and standards that govern his new role. Second, he must have the sheer **ability** to perform adequately. This includes the capacity to learn and utilize new skills appropriately to meet expectations. Thus, one basic assumption in

---

11. Orville Brim and Stanton Wheeler, *op. cit.*, p. 25.

socialization is that, for any given objective, performance must not be unacceptably limited by deficiencies of either endowment or training. Finally, the trainee must have sufficient **motivation.** He simply has to have enough incentive and willingness to perform acceptably. Presumably all three conditions are necessary for effective socialization to any role, whether in formal organizations or informal structures, whether in primary or secondary groups. Of the three factors, motivation may be the most problematic in many contexts, and socialization may fail more because of disinterest than ineptitude.

To be sure, socialization without positive motivation is feasible, as in the coercive prototype of George Orwell's *1984.* Under some conditions it is possible to secure conformity and identification and to inculcate values against a trainee's will, even in the face of his active opposition. This is apparent from concentration camp experiences and attempts at brainwashing in the Korean war.[12] Such efforts are less successful when trainees may resign or when they have strong group supports in resisting indoctrination, but are more successful when trainees are not sustained by a group.[13] Generally, while raw coercion may be effective, it usually varies with individuals and often produces limited, imperfect socialization with many gaps. Less coercive situations may also counteract adverse motivation, eventually securing a trainee's voluntary commitment and a change in his values. Thus, a person who is placed in a conflict between his desires

---

12. Bruno Bettelheim, "Individual and Mass Behavior in Extreme Situations," *Journal of Abnormal and Social Psychology,* 38 (1943) 417–52; Albert Biderman, "The Image of 'Brainwashing,'" *Public Opinion Quarterly,* 26 (1962) 547–63; Edgar Schein, *Coercive Persuasion* (New York: W. W. Norton, 1961).

13. George Grosser, "The Role of Informal Inmate Groups in Change of Values," *Children,* 5 (January–February, 1958) 25–29; Roland Wulbert, "Inmate Pride in Total Institutions," *American Journal of Sociology,* 71 (1965) 1–9.

and action may resolve the strain by ultimately changing his beliefs to make them consistent with his behavior.[14]

But, in the present context, negative motivation cannot always be overcome in the effort to socialize people to stigmatic roles. Cogswell, for example, describes the efforts to rehabilitate paraplegics and prepare them for those limitations that their injury imposes on their future lives.[15] With understandable strain, most of the patients were eventually brought to the point of accepting the reality of their paralysis and the cognitive restructuring that this entailed. Similarly, most could be successfully brought through the intensive training program in which they mastered new physical skills —handling their bodies, motor control, movement, and so on. But only a few were successful in adapting to the *social* situations they had to face in undertaking a seminormal, relatively independent life in the community. Of the twenty-six patients intensively studied, only six returned to any kind of work at all—not necessarily to their previous occupations, but simply to jobs that they were capable of performing. However, for the other twenty, the advantages and independence of a job were not enough to offset the painful stigma of being severely crippled. Though their knowledge and ability were both adequate, their motivation was too weak. Thus, they were physically but not socially rehabilitated: they preferred withdrawal to socialization.

Apparently the aged do not suffer as much of a handicap or stigma as the paralyzed,[16] but their prospective socialization is equally tenuous. In Brim and Wheeler's terms, the old may have the necessary ability to be socialized, but their

---

14. Leon Festinger, *A Theory of Cognitive Dissonance* (Evanston: Row, Peterson, 1957).

15. Betty Cogswell, "Rehabilitation of the Paraplegic: Processes of Socialization," *Sociological Inquiry*, 37 (Winter, 1967) 11–26.

16. John Tringo, "The Hierarchy of Preference Toward Disability Groups," *Journal of Special Education*, 4 (1970) 295–306.

knowledge and motivation are both drastically impaired. The vague norms preclude clear knowledge and standards for ordering their lives. With no significant compensation for their social losses, they have little incentive to embrace old age, and their motives are understandably weak. As motivation declines, the normal socialization forces correspondingly lose force. These are not intensified because the results are not vital to the society, and thus there is little interest in raising the social investment in the process. In addition, the emotional resistance of the aged, intensified by their demoralization and their sense of powerlessness to govern their own fate, seriously impairs cognitive processes and their ability to learn new role-relevant information.[17] Thus, weak motives blunt normal socialization forces and remain a crucial factor in later life.

THE DENIAL OF OLD AGE

This low motivation is directly reflected in old people's systematic denial that they are aged. This is one of the most stable, consistently documented findings reported in the gerontological literature.[18] Basically, older persons share the common denigrating beliefs about the elderly, but only about others. They exempt themselves personally from such invidious social judgments. Thus, they stigmatize others while resolutely dissociating themselves from the stigmatized category. For example, in my own study of the aged, only one-third of the sample regarded persons over sixty-five as still

17. Herbert McCloskey and John Schaar, "Psychological Dimensions of Anomy," *American Sociological Review*, 30 (1965) 14–40; Melvin Seeman, "Alienation and Social Learning in a Reformatory," *American Journal of Sociology*, 69 (1963) 270–83; Melvin Seeman and John Evans, "Alienation and Learning in a Hospital Setting," *American Sociological Review*, 27 (1962) 772–82.

18. A detailed review of the relevant literature appears in Irving Rosow, *Social Integration of the Aged*, esp. pp. 30–35 and 252–61.

productive and useful, but fully five-sixths felt that they were still useful themselves. Similarly, while five-sixths agreed that older persons who denied that they were old were "usually just kidding themselves," more than one-half then insisted that they personally were not old.[19] To be sure, there are perceptible differences in the propensity to deny, with a direct relationship between social losses and subsequent denial. When they are old, middle-class persons suffer more deprivation than members of the working class *relative to their middle-age standards*. Accordingly, our middle-class sample was significantly more likely than working-class respondents to deny losses of prestige, despite the clear withering away of any objective evidence for their beliefs.[20] But such differences are only a refinement of the more general problem. That the denial is psychologically defensive is also secondary, for it represents an effort to mitigate real, not imaginary, consequences.[21] Basically, such denial exposes a sharp discrepancy between self-conceptions and social definitions that generate strain[22] and complicate any prospective socialization.

The aged, of course, are not the only ones who try to exempt themselves from invidious positions or stigmatic judgments. Members of low-caste groups, for example, always recognize a clear caste structure with definite norms, but commonly deny its legitimacy or their own classification within it.[23] The crippled and handicapped often manipulate interaction with normal persons as if they were not impaired

---

19. *Ibid.*, p. 260.

20. Ibid., pp. 278–85.

21. Cf. Derek Phillips, "Rejection: A Possible Consequence of Seeking Help for Mental Disorders," *American Sociological Review*, 28 (1963) 963–72.

22. Caroline Preston and Karen Gudiksen, "A Measure of Self-Perception Among Older People," *Journal of Gerontology*, 21 (1966) 63–71.

23. F. G. Bailey, "Closed Social Stratification in India," *European Journal of Sociology*, 4 (1963) 107–24; Gerald Berreman, "Caste in India and the United States," *American Journal of Sociology*, 66 (1960) 120–27.

and there were no special condition of the relationship.[24] They simply deny reality. This differs from the caste example, for the disabled try to impose normal definitions of themselves on situations that are ambiguous precisely because there are few norms about appropriate behavior toward the disabled. This applies not only to the physically handicapped, but also to other deviants, such as the dying or those getting a divorce a generation ago, cases marked by a similar ambiguity of expectations and behavior.[25] Hence, the aged are only one of many groups attempting to deal with stigmatic definitions, but they have no corresponding norms to guide their relationships. As others do, they commonly resort to denial, and this creates a tension between their pretences and social perceptions of them.

When action is based on different conceptions of reality, the fundamental problem is really one of consensus.[26] The discrepancy between self- and others' images of the aged can be quite consequential, for it breaks down a shared basis of understanding and communication, and thus the common meaning of acts and the predictability of response.[27] Such divergent views are also significant for old people's social identity.[28] For disparagement of a person's deviance has less effect on his self-esteem and adaptation than does *agreement*

---

24. Fred Davis, "Deviance Disavowal: The Management of Strained Interaction by the Visibly Handicapped," *Social Problems*, 9 (Winter, 1961) 120–32.

25. Barney Glaser and Anselm Strauss, "Temporal Aspects of Dying as a Non-Scheduled Status Passage," *American Journal of Sociology*, 71 (1965) 48–59; William Goode, *After Divorce* (Glencoe: Free Press, 1956).

26. Bernice Neugarten, Joan Moore and John Lowe, "Age Norms, Age Constraints, and Adult Socialization," *American Journal of Sociology*, 70 (1965) 710–17.

27. Kenneth Eckhardt and Gerry Hendershot, "Dissonance, Congruence and the Perception of Public Opinion," *American Journal of Sociology*, 73 (1967) 222–34; Thomas Scheff, "Towards a Sociological Model of Consensus," *American Sociological Review*, 32 (1967) 32–46.

28. Barney Glaser and Anselm Strauss, "Awareness Contexts and Social Interaction," *American Sociological Review*, 29 (1964) 669–79.

about his status, whatever that status might be.[29] Certainly, the prospect for successful socialization to any role, but particularly to any devalued status, including aging, is directly related to the degree of consensus between actor and agents.

STRUCTURE OF SOCIALIZATION SITUATIONS

We have seen that norms for older people tend to be vague and that this fact presumably militates against socialization. But such ambiguity is not typical of all socialization situations. The goals of training may not always be fully explicit and consensual; but usually there is reasonable clarity and working agreement on major objectives. This is particularly true in virtually all formal settings, such as in the army or professional schools, which train and indoctrinate candidates for a new role. The institutional patterns are highly structured by analytic elements that govern socialization. Their functions can usually be related to socialization objectives, or to the output of a definite social product.

On the other hand, informal socialization tends to be much less structured. Informal contexts may have more diffuse boundaries to the socialization field, less formal rules and regulations, more implicit standards and expectations, and generally subtler and vaguer elements. For example, learning the norms of a husband's role may require many relationships and experiences, possibly even a larger role set, all of which cut across several situations rather than being confined within a single setting, as training in an academy would be. Thus, the crucial variables in socialization tend to be much clearer and more visible in formal situations than they are in informal situations.

However, and we shall address this later, the point is not simply to distinguish the two situations by definition, for this

29. Barbara Lorch, "The Perception of Deviancy by Self and Others," *Sociology and Social Research*, 50 (1966) 223–29.

has only limited value. The important distinctions are not mainly definitional. The real issue is to identify the similarities and differences in the two situations and to clarify their significance for socialization, with particular attention to their functional equivalence. This is based on the assumption that, however deceptive their external forms, functionally comparable factors probably govern both contexts. Thus, even though formal and informal settings seem to have different properties, they may still produce similar socialization results, with different mechanisms having rather comparable effects. This does not imply an *identity* of function, but only the likelihood of major similarities. This is a significant problem to be clarified in future research.

Accordingly, we shall try to identify the possible similarities and differences between formal and informal socialization settings. The similarities are most likely to inhere in the most general elements of the socialization field, for its framework provides the properties through which the socialization process operates. Specifying these structural properties will enable us to judge the adequacy for socialization of the life conditions of most older people.

The structural elements and the crucial socialization variables tend to be more sharply delineated in formal than informal settings. So we will first examine the formal training situation as a prototype of the relatively complete socialization field that contains all the significant factors. Presumably, similar elements should also operate in informal situations, but possibly not in all of them. Later on we will consider the major differences in the two situations. Thus, we are concerned not only with training for work and bureaucratic positions, but also with other roles, including old age, which are learned informally. However, the structural elements themselves are of first importance, and we will now examine them in formal situations.

The formal training situation is typically structured in

the form of an inverted "T". This consists of a vertical axis of authority groups, or socializers, and a horizontal base of peers, or trainees. These comprise the trainee's minimal reference and membership groups in the situation, and they reflect the distribution of authority and competence in the system. The authority of the socializers rests on both their formal responsibility and their technical qualification. They not only have superior knowledge, they also have power over the trainee, judging, testing, rewarding and disciplining him. The novice, on the other hand, normally enters at the bottom of the hierarchy, inexperienced, relatively incompetent, with few prerogatives and a maximum of dependence. Many special practices, such as fraternity hazing, symbolically express his inferior position. Aside from qualifying him for recruitment, the trainee's previous experience, achievement, or place in life supposedly do not affect his initial rank in the socialization hierarchy. His formal status is characterized by the dependence, social regression, and lack of expertise of the novice or apprentice.

Clearly, this situation may generate anxiety, the severity of which varies with the recruits, the institution, the recruitment and training programs, and the importance to the novices of the positions for which they are being trained. Such anxiety, however, may usefully motivate them to learn, to perform, and to internalize the norms and values.

Role Models

Authorities and peers are complementary sources of role models for the trainee. Ideally, the authorities constitute rather *complete* or finished models for identification. To this extent, they can be not only a positive reference group, but also a set of ideal images for the post-training period. In this sense, they are models primarily for *future* roles and only secondarily for the training process, for the students' problems in regard to learning and adapting are quite different from their mentors'.[30]

On the other hand, the peer group is also a rich source of models, one of *contemporary* significance. They provide models for current adaptation to the position of trainees in meeting *training* demands effectively, in clarifying expectations and performance standards, techniques of mastery, competence, etc. In this sense, peers are models for *present* role fulfillment. In grossly oversimplified terms, the authority group personifies the *goals* of socialization while the peer group provides many of the *means* of current adaptation.[31]

These two types of role model have different time referents and ultimately different role referents. To be sure, both roles represent stages in a coherent status sequence and share many norms.[32] But normative differences do occur, and behavior that may be acceptable in the earlier stage may no longer be appropriate later.[33] This is not surprising insofar as each period has its own problems and standards of competence, responsibility, and authority. The varying expectations inhere in the differences between learning and finished performance, between role-taking and role-playing.[34] In other words, there is apparently a built-in possibility of some role conflict between present and future norms. But ordinarily this is not problematic during the training period. Even though the learning pressures may favor the adoption of trainee norms, this certainly does not preclude the simul-

30. Robert Merton, George Reader and Patricia Kendall, *The Student-Physician* (Cambridge: Harvard University Press, 1957).

31. Robert Rapoport, Rhona Rapoport and Irving Rosow, *Community as Doctor* (London: Tavistock, 1960) 197–201.

32. Robert Merton, *Social Theory and Social Structure*, rev. ed. (Glencoe: Free Press, 1957) 368–86; Robert Merton, George Reader and Patricia Kendall, *op. cit.*

33. Howard Becker and Blanche Geer, "The Fate of Idealism in Medical School," *American Sociological Review*, 23 (1958) 50–56.

34. Walter Coutu, "Role-Playing vs. Role-Taking," *American Sociological Review*, 16 (1951) 180–87.

taneous learning of post-training standards. Both are absorbed; they simply receive a different priority in application. If they should conflict, trainee norms take precedence during socialization, while the more fundamental norms apply after training. This is quite marked in medicine, where an apparently cynical, flippant student culture predominates in medical school and then gives way to a more sober professional demeanor when the young physician enters practice.[35] Similarly, norms at the onset of marriage are modified by the arrival of children. But in these cases, the early stages anticipate the later and preclude any basic role discontinuity.[36]

There is fragmentary and inconclusive evidence that peers may exert even greater influence on trainees' future role conceptions than theory would predict.[37] This does not mean that the peer group literally provides its own future role models—these usually do originate in the authority group (or in outside surrogates). But the peer group's *evaluation* of authority models strongly influences its members' preferences. For, just as authorities rate students, so do trainees rate teachers and thereby affect the choice of models. By channeling identification differentially, the peer group mediates between present and future roles, between conceptions and behavior, between orientation and effective values. Thereby, it moderates its members' high dependence and low power and makes for some flexibility in the alternatives available to them.[38]

Further, trainees do not depend solely on their teachers for future role models. This varies according to external ties

35. Howard Becker and Blanche Geer, *op. cit.*
36. Ruth Benedict, "Continuities and Discontinuities in Cultural Conditioning," *Psychiatry*, 1 (1938) 161–67.
37. Robert Coker, *et al.*, "Patterns of Influence: Medical School Faculty Members and the Values and Specialty Interests of Medical Students," *Journal of Medical Education*, 35 (1960) 518–27.
38. Richard Emerson, "Power-Dependence Relations," *American Sociological Review*, 27 (1962) 31–41.

of individuals and to the isolation of the socialization field. Role models in the authority group may be vitiated by reference figures outside the training situation. Such external groups may provide the trainee with alternative norms or supports, thereby reducing his dependence in the socialization setting and probably his vulnerability to its standards and pressures. To illustrate, "closed" institutions—such as prisons, monasteries, military academies or sanatoria—drastically limit their new members' outside contacts. External ties are effectively cut, which tends to focus the trainees' major reference groups within the system. This is in contrast to such open settings as families or to loosely bounded organizations where external contact and influence are routine and often quite high. For example, physicians may work for private corporations, and adolescents may belong to their peer cliques. Their participation within open contexts (corporation or family) may be strongly affected by their external associations (profession or clique). These outside contacts may certainly provide a source of role models which may conflict with those within the field.

Accordingly, the less bounded and sealed the training field *and* the more contact with potential models outside, the greater both the trainee's autonomy and the prospect of conflicting role models. Conversely, the more encapsulated the training and the fewer his external links, the greater his dependence and the less his likelihood of alternative models. The critical factor in the relative isolation of the field, however, is its effect in increasing either the recruit's autonomy or dependence in the socialization setting.

External reference groups reinforce the effects of socializing agents when their values cohere. But this becomes extremely problematic when trainees identify with outside role models whose values or norms *conflict with those of internal authority figures.* For this vitiates the effects of the formal socializing agents.

Four conditions are favorable to the orientation to external models: (1) Trainees may be relatively independent of teachers for opportunities after training. Their access to future positions reduces their dependence on internal sponsors and limits it to the training period itself. Their future prospects are not decisively affected by their compliance and by their mentors' goodwill.[39] Thus, independent opportunities ease the situational pressures for strong identification with an internal figure and increase the relative chances of an orientation to external role models.

(2) Periods of sharp political and social conflict may align many trainees with outside reference figures who may substantially discredit formal socializing agents as legitimate models. Teachers may be seen as technically competent, but symbolic of moribund values; perhaps useful for learning skills, but unqualified as social philosophers; temporarily acceptable for teaching means, but not ends; and, generally, as socially obsolete. Such trainee perspectives typically rest on strong external group supports that reduce the dependence on socialization authorities for future opportunities and discourage identification with them as role models.

This condition is exemplified in the recent militancy of university students who have strong group ties with off-campus political movements. Similarly, it appears in social revolutions that seek pervasive change of major institutions, power elites, and central values—as in the promises of all totalitarian regimes of sweeping reforms borne on the wings of a revolutionary generation. Less extreme perhaps are the young medical students who are genuinely committed to an ideal of socialized medicine and repudiate their professors' conception of the doctor's traditional role; lacking sympathe-

---

39. Irving Rosow, "Affluence, Reciprocity and Solidary Bonds," paper prepared for the Biennial Meeting of the International Society for the Study of Behavioral Development: Ann Arbor, August, 1973. (publication pending)

tic models, they are obliged to project idealized models on which to pattern themselves. These are special cases of competing reference groups from which trainees draw on external figures to fashion models in the image of their ideological commitments.

These patterns are directly related to external events. They are different from those in which trainees fabricate their own role models because of conflict with authorities which has nothing to do with social change and outside reference groups. For example, despite exceptions,[40] prisoners do not model themselves after guards because the two groups are basically inimical to each other. Instead, prisoners generate their own exemplars as an affirmation of integrity and group values (viz., toughness).[41] To be sure, this may reflect basic animosities rather than literal value conflicts, for the fundamental value differences between convicts and their keepers may be tenuous indeed. But in this case, external models are not significant, as they are when larger social change impinges directly on role modeling and socialization.

(3) Authority figures may also be weak role models when they simply teach, but do *not* demonstrate the actual *practice* of a future role. That is, they are truncated rather than complete exponents of the range of competence the trainee will presumably master. This has two components. First, teachers who do not demonstrate techniques to students do not display the full repertoire of *skills* encompassed in a role. Hence, they are inadequate as models. For example, retired or unsuccessful athletic coaches or ballet, dramatic, and art teachers may not be able to demonstrate effectively the required skills and techniques they are trying to transmit.

---

40. Bruno Bettelheim, *op. cit.*; LaMar Empey and Jerome Rabow, "The Provo Experiment in Delinquency Rehabilitation," *American Sociological Review*, 26 (1961) 679–95.

41. Stanton Wheeler, "Socialization in Correctional Communities," *American Sociological Review*, 26 (1961) 697–712.

Consequently, they may invoke for emulation, often through pictures or films, the image of distinguished virtuosi—Ted Williams' swing, Margot Fonteyn's pirouette, Judith Anderson's power, or Botticelli's line. But failure to demonstrate properly means incomplete modeling. Second, teachers who do not also practice do not display the full range of *attitudes and interaction* with the entire future role set. They may associate with some significant others, but simply tell students about relations with them. So the trainees have no direct exposure to and opportunity to observe directly how these relationships are structured and properly handled. Aside from possible misrepresentations by the teacher, they are thrown back on their imagination to flesh out relationships in areas where they are inexperienced. Such modeling is also incomplete.

We can identify relatively complete and truncated models in professional education by contrasting medical with social work training. When medical students do rounds with mentor physicians and instructors in hospital wards, clinics, or laboratories, their image of the role set, the professional relationships and the norms is complete and integrated in one coherent conception. In contrast, social work education divorces classroom instruction from field work practice in community agencies. The school faculty teaches principles of practice, but does not demonstrate professional skills in working directly with clients and colleagues. Consequently, there is a succession of fragmentary or partial role models, often lacking coherence, consistency, and clarity. The division of "role-model labor" among several incomplete figures militates against role clarity and easy student identification with instructors. Hence, they may create ideal role models, synthesized from imagination or portions of actual figures in classrooms or agencies where they are assigned for field training. Becker and Carper describe also the relative ineffectiveness of philosophy professors as direct role models for their

graduate students who cannot delineate a clear role conception from their mentors' activities.[42] After all, aside from lec-
tures and seminars, their teachers sit at a desk and read, think,
and write. But in terms of substance and process, what do
their activities entail? What and how do they think and write?
In this case, individual and peer group definitions become
most important in muddling through to a vague set of expectations. These may even resemble their professors' activities superficially, though not necessarily in substance. Any
resemblance is often purely adventitious rather than the result of effective direct modeling, whether conscious or not.

(4) Outside persons may become models when they
control immediate opportunities and rewards to which trainees may have access *during* training. This is a variation of the
first condition. Kadushin offers an interesting analysis of the
emerging professional self-image of music students.[43] His research found no change of values during their years in the
conservatory, presumably because they had previously assimilated the appropriate beliefs as a result of anticipatory
socialization. Hence, their teachers had comparatively little
effect on those values Kadushin examined. However, their
self-conceptions as *professionals* varied significantly with
several factors in the course of their training. By far the most
important of these was whether or not students performed
for pay, usually in orchestras or ensembles. To the extent that
they engaged in public performances, they regarded themselves as professional musicians. Such free-lance students
commonly have to join the musicians' union to secure even
spot jobs.

---

42. Howard Becker and James Carper, "The Development of Identification with an Occupation," *American Journal of Sociology*, 61 (1956)
289–98, and "The Elements of Identification with an Occupation," *American Sociological Review*, 21 (1956) 341–48.
43. Charles Kadushin, "The Professional Self-Concept of Music
Students," *American Journal of Sociology*, 75 (1969) 398–404.

This pattern was subject to several conditions that typify some, but not all, socialization processes. Opportunities for students were located in a free talent market independent of the conservatory. Informal links between the two may have affected, but did not determine, access to employment. The distribution of jobs made no concession to a performer's student status, but was governed by his talent as a professional musician. Finally, the standards of judgment were those of the employing orchestra, not the student's teachers. These outside employers were, of course, musicians themselves. Insofar as they regulated immediate and prospective opportunities, students were extremely responsive to their standards and norms. Many of them who controlled recurrent engagements and could offer a series of part-time slots were strategically situated to become significant models for most professional students. Thus, the more talented students functioned simultaneously in two independent fields: the conservatory and the professional labor market. As a socialization arena, the school was certainly clear-cut and sharply bounded, but not isolated. Therefore, the boundary of the field was permeable, and the most qualified students were open to outside influence as a function of the external opportunities. This situation differs from all training that culminates in formal qualification, certification, or licensing procedures. The practice of emerging professional skills is closely regulated and supervised. No matter how capable, students of medicine, law, pharmacy, nursing, and other professions do not achieve full professional status and are not permitted to practice independently or to freelance until they have passed their board exams or the equivalent. Thus, their sequential statuses as student and professional are sharply demarcated from each other. But in the case of music and other roles in which the criteria of competence are not formalized, the stages in a career are not equally differentiated. Then there may be considerable overlap between earlier and later periods, between

novice and socially mature roles. Accordingly, the transition
between stages may be easier and more fluid simply by virtue
of role playing. Certainly the fuzziness between stages makes
the transition process vaguer and less perceptible. But, by the
same token, the identity of the most appropriate role models
may also be more flexible and indefinite. Thereby, outside
opportunities during training may stimulate external role
models, increasingly so as the most professionally competent
students advance through the program.

In all four conditions, the trainee's sheer *dependence* on
authority figures is reduced, and his orientation to potential
outside models is facilitated. But, except under special circumstances, this is rather unusual. Normally, dependence on
the system is maintained. Socializing agents usually prefer
internal models and strongly discourage orientation to external figures, especially to deviants. However, as we shall
see later on, in terms of the elderly there are not only few
effective models within their primary groups, but also a serious dearth outside. This presents a significant obstacle to
their socialization.

Stratification of the Peer Group

We have described the structure of the socialization situation in the form of an inverted "T", consisting of a vertical
authority group and a horizontal base of peers. One crucial
feature of this structure is the *stratification of the trainee
group*.[44] These strata follow two general axes: advancement
and excellence. *Advancement* differentiates trainees according to their progress through the formal curriculum or program. By this token, it orders students along a continuum,
separating upper classmen from lower classmen, those who

---

44. The parallel differentiation of the authority group also raises
another set of major theoretical problems. But these are peripheral to the
socialization of older people and are not considered here.

have completed various requirements and qualifications tests from those who have not; in brief, the more advanced from the less advanced. On the other hand, *excellence* recognizes outstanding individual merit, either informally or by rewarding distinguished performance with various honors. This may take diverse forms, including honor rolls, honor societies, and fellowships or coveted awards, usually competitive. Where higher stages are valued because of the amount of training and growing competence they represent, honors are prestigious because they indicate personal superiority and quality.

Both axes of stratification rank trainees on their relative status. The most successful group members clarify role expectations by personifying the criteria of ranking. Thereby, the central norms lose some abstraction and become more concrete, embodied as they are in pecr models for emulation. This serves a cognitive function, for the emphasis of standards through personification fosters common norms and role definitions.

Further, both advancement and excellence reinforce growing identification with roles to which one is increasingly committed. The stratification symbolizes greater competence and qualification to take on new responsibilities. Role playing not only develops progressively on a quasiapprenticeship basis *during* training—as in medical students' regular ward rounds or law students' mock court trials or graduate students' supervision of research assistants. But also, the more advanced trainees thereby become authority *surrogates* and partial role models for those who are less experienced.[45] The stratification thus places higher trainees in an *intermediate* position in the system, and they help to bridge the gap between the highest authority and the lowest trainee levels. The peer group's interpretation of their mentors' expectations be-

---

45. LaMar Empey and Jerome Rabow, *op. cit.*

comes a crucial link in the transmission of norms to the inexperienced novices.[46] Thereby, the higher trainees provide
informal (sometimes formal) leadership and become the
strategic middlemen in the larger system. The growing competence, authority, responsibility, and commitment of the
more advanced trainees reinforces and deepens their own
identification with the role.

Goal-Gradients

But the most generalized function of peer stratification
is the creation of *goal-gradients*. The different statuses have
two effects. First, they rank individuals and groups by their
stage of training or advancement. This breaks down the
larger program into smaller steps or subsections of manage-
able proportions that the trainee can successfully master.
This reduces the long-range, sometimes abstract and remote
goals into programmatic sequences that he can more readily
grasp. In other words, the comprehensive program, which in
its entirety may be forbidding, even awesome, is ordered into
a series of separate, bite-size chunks that can be handled.
These specify immediate expectations and requirements in
concrete terms that orient and direct the trainee and clearly
indicate his responsibilities in any given period. To this extent, they represent a series of discrete subgoals that break
up the total program into a set of gradients. Hence, goal-
gradients.

The second effect of status differences is to give all trainees an objective check on their progress. They can assess their
own performance relative to others and place themselves with
reasonable accuracy on both stratification axes of the peer
group. Hence, the goal-gradients are reference points for self-

---

46. Howard Becker and James Carper, "The Development of Identification with an Occupation," esp. 292.

evaluation. Thus, the comparisons indicate that higher peers are a likely reference group for those in lower ranks.[47]

In summary, the subgoals serve to locate the person in the socialization system on the two major status dimensions: advancement and excellence. They clarify the trainee's place in the system according to his quality of performance and his progress toward the overall training goals.

Insofar as the criteria for both ratings are intrinsically clear, partially competitive, and reasonably objective, they sharpen the structure of formal socialization situations. While similar evaluations may operate in informal socialization, they cannot be nearly as definitive. Role performance is easier to assess objectively, for example, in the case of a professional student than in the case of a husband. Because the prospective socialization to old age is largely concentrated in informal settings, we will now compare formal and informal socialization situations.

FORMAL AND INFORMAL SOCIALIZATION

Because the transition to *devalued* statuses can mobilize only weak motives, the differences between formal and informal structures are critical for socialization. The formal situation can often overcome weak incentives or even resistance, so that a person will accept an inferior position and evaluation. But without compelling socializing pressures, the informal situation requires the trainee's voluntary compliance for his effective socialization.

We may define *formal* socialization as a specific training program of a formal organization designed to induct per-

---

47. Howard Becker and James Carper, *ibid.;* Harold Kelley, "Two Functions of Reference Groups," in Guy Swanson, Theodore Newcomb and Eugene Hartley (eds.), *Readings in Social Psychology*, rev. ed. (New York: Holt, 1952) 410–14.

sons into a role or group. The training is purposive, intended to result in a definite social product: a person of particular skills and beliefs. The major objectives and procedures are usually specified, though often in quite general terms. Responsibility for training is clearly designated. Examples of this approach include army camps, professional schools, academies, apprenticeship programs, or other institutions that formally prepare inductees for new positions. In contrast, *informal* socialization tends to be much less structured on all these counts, certainly in its context and external forms. Though organizations include informal mechanisms, purely informal socialization fields are not set in organizations. Objectives are seldom explicit and procedures are all informal, with responsibility not sharply allocated. Examples of this approach include the introduction to friendship groups, learning to be a spouse, and so on. Hence, formal and informal socialization tend to occur under quite different conditions.

These differences consist of two related elements: structure and process. Socialization may be formalized in both its organizational context and in its training mechanisms. Conversely, it may be informal in both, as, for example, when a bunch of friends gradually break in a newcomer to the group. But they may also be combined: informal processes invariably become vital socializing mechanisms within formal institutions, and the fact that they are common to both settings contributes to some confusion. The informal mechanisms in formal organizations tend to blur the differences between the two contexts, while the structural features tend to emphasize them.

The crucial factor, however, is not simply definitional or classificatory. Rather, it is necessary to specify those features of formal and informal settings that would seem to strengthen or weaken the socializing pressures. For this purpose, it is essential to clarify the major structural differences that commonly distinguish the two contexts. While an exhaustive list might be longer, the most important differences include the following factors:

(1) Formal organizations are usually **larger** than informal groups, with more people and sundry institutional impedimenta at all levels. More trainees are being processed at any time, often more impersonally and not so closely as in small, informal groups.

(2) Formal situations are the more **highly structured.** Recruitment, initiation to and separation from formal institutions follow objective procedures and meet specific criteria. These tend to be less systematic and controlled in informal contexts. The goals of formal organizations are more explicit, conscious, and purposive than in informal settings. Rules, training procedures, and the mechanics of socialization are also more organized in formal situations and are looser or vaguer in the informal. Similarly, formal situations more often operate with clearer standards and expectations, reinforced by objective performance criteria and ratings.

(3) In formal settings, **roles are defined** in a division of labor, authority and responsibility more clearly than in informal situations, and the resulting social structure is typically more institutionalized and stable. The organization of positions constitutes a framework for the continuity of the system, and the maintenance of functions often compensates for the weakness of strategically located persons and even of leadership failure. However, small, informal groups are specifically vulnerable to personal shortcomings and generally sensitive to the personality of their members.[48] Formal institutions may suffer demoralization, friction, or inefficiency because of their members' personal characteristics (quite apart from the bureaucratic culture), but nonetheless they can survive strains that would destroy informal groups. Thus, aside from common objectives that integrate structures, in-

48. Irving Rosow, "Issues in the Concept of Need Complementarity," *Sociometry,* 20 (1957) 216–33.

formal settings depend on and are sensitive to personal com-
patibility, while formal situations rely more on impersonal
norms and role expectations.

(4) While both situations emphasize the importance of
behavioral and attitudinal changes, the formal include technical skills and knowledge that may be ancillary or absent in
informal groups. Formal training generally concentrates on
instrumental purposes, while the informal also commonly
stresses the expressive. Hence, in formal socialization, group
membership is typically a means to other ends, while in informal settings membership is more often an end in itself. Consequently, different time perspectives often prevail, especially
in relation to the future. Trainees in formal socialization settings tend to see their membership as temporary and finite, as
one stage in a set of status sequences that make present peer
groups transitory and instable. But in informal settings, the
future is commonly regarded as open-ended, with an implicit
assumption of group continuity and the relative stability of
membership.

(5) Formal situations are typically, though not invariably, **complete, bounded, and self-contained.** They usually
contain all the components of the inverted "T" model. In
contrast, informal settings may be incomplete, lacking elements that are dispersed over *several* situations. This makes
the informal socialization field dependent on complementary external inputs which must be processed and integrated.
Such integration is seldom a controlled, coherent procedure,
but is often subject to adventitious factors.

This can be illustrated by contrasting almost any formal
professional training with acquiring the role and norms of a
spouse. Although becoming a husband or wife involves much
anticipatory socialization, this only becomes a base for subsequent development in the course of the marriage. Whereas
professional training provides all the ingredients for socialization, the marriage specifically does not include: (a) a dis-

tinctive authority group, (b) a peer group in the *same* status as the actor, and (c) role models for that position. Substitutes may be found *outside* the marriage, especially role models. Friends or acquaintances, kin or siblings, parents or other elders all represent potential substitutes for the missing peers and role models. But there is no viable authority capable of systematic appraisal and control through sanctions and approval.

This incomplete arrangement has two significant weaknesses for effective socialization. First, the novice must integrate the diverse external sources himself, without the guides that are built into a formal situation. Second, these independent sources represent several potential reference groups. As their number multiplies, the chances increase that their norms will conflict; therefore the likelihood of role confusion rather than clarity. In contrast, the formal situation generally presses toward consensus and clearer expectations. Most informal socialization, however, is not involved with major roles such as that of the spouse, but simply with informal group memberships such as friendship circles. This is especially true for the aged among their friends, neighbors, and similar associates, commonly peers. And as these groups suffer attrition, their viable socialization resources tend to dwindle.

(6) When a set of peers constitutes the *complete* informal socialization field, this fuses the formal situation's authority and peer groups into one. Authority functions are divided between: (a) the peer leadership and (2) the general group norms. Such authority may be powerful and coercive, as with adolescent cliques and gangs or the politesse of exclusive friendship circles. When the group is open and its membership voluntary (even though members might function is if they were not), its authority ultimately depends on group attractiveness, solidarity, and cohesion precisely because membership and conformity *are* voluntary, and control

is thereby limited. Consequently, effective authority is restricted by the importance of the group to its members and
their goals and by the alternative groups open to them. If its
importance is not high and if attractive alternatives are available, the member's dependence is low and the group's authority is tenuous or weak.[49] In contrast, authority in formal
settings does not depend fundamentally on group attractiveness and member satisfaction, but on the legitimacy of the
institution and its **control** over the trainee's fate. The latter
might be limited because of alternatives available to him elsewhere, but this is highly variable between settings. This is
particularly important for the aged, whose position, especially if they are rather isolated, tends to be vulnerable. Because the aged tend to have few attractive alternatives, their
informal group memberships may be quite fragile. So they
may be quite dependent on a group for association and, therefore, amenable to its authority and pressures. However, the
sheer fact of their dependence in no way determines the particular norms or values that might be implemented by possible group pressures.

(7) Formal situations are also probably subject to
greater **ideal-real discrepancies** than the informal. The sheer
size and formality of its program and norms tend to make the
formal situation less flexible than the informal in adapting to
external changes, new conditions, or requirements. Indeed,
the stability of large bureaucratic structures largely depends
on their informal systems to provide the initial flexibility
needed to meet new or irregular situations. The problem of
flexibility is intensified to the extent that formal training is
instrumental, often servicing the changing needs of outside
institutions—as in most cases of higher education. In contrast, informal systems are considerably more flexible and
adaptable, aided by smaller size and often by the prominence

---

49. Richard Emerson, *op. cit.*

of expressive ends. Consequently, the gap between professed and observed standards is likely to be less. In informal systems, the real approximates the ideal more closely than in formal settings.

(8) Competition among peers probably has different effects on their **solidarity** in the two situations. In the formal group, competition is directed toward limited rewards whose scarcity makes striving endemic. One result of this competition, of course, is to fix relative peer statuses in the prestige hierarchy. But, because tests and ratings recur periodically, making positions subject to change, competition also becomes chronic. Therefore, it is primarily divisive in the peer group, pitting individuals, cliques, and subgroups against each other.[50] In the informal group, competition also serves the status- or power-fixing function. Once this is established, it defines relative status, clarifies group structure, and stabilizes the relations among members. Competitive tests become irregular and infrequent; competitive pressures are less sustained, chronic, and divisive. Thus, group support should be a more stable feature of informal than of formal situations.

(9) Both settings generate a functional anxiety that is conducive to socialization of trainees. Objects of anxiety are probably more focused in the formal situation and more diffuse in the informal. Also, **anxiety levels** may commonly be higher in the formal than in the informal because the trainee's institutional commitments are usually more clear-cut.[51] This is paralleled by the formal situation's more structured mechanisms that tend to reduce anxiety. Explicit expectations, performance tests, formal ratings, and similar techniques allow the trainee to evaluate himself and clarify his objective stand-

50. L. Keith Miller and Robert Hamblin, "Interdependence, Differential Rewarding and Productivity," *American Sociological Review*, 28 (1963) 768–78.

51. Howard Becker, "Notes on the Concept of Commitment," *American Journal of Sociology*, 66 (1960) 32–40, and "Personal Change in Adult Life," *Sociometry*, 27 (1964) 40–53.

ing. Thereby, he can construe clearly both the situation and his relation to it. This gives a reality base to the changes in self-image which attend socialization. In contrast, informal situations contain few equivalents of these, but instead operate with more implicit and adumbrated cues for the resolution of any ambiguities in the situation. While informal mechanisms may function successfully, the resolution of anxiety is not so patterned. To the extent that reality checks are limited, this allows freer play to that perceptual distortion which sustains anxiety.

(10) Other things being equal, there is probably a difference in the relative **depth and quality of socialization** produced by the two situations. The informal is more likely to result in *fuller internalization* of values, while the formal engenders more *simulated* socialization.[52] In the formal setting, conditions allow substantial concealment of deviant values and beliefs if one chooses. Sheer numbers limit both the frequency of the trainee's contact with socializing authorities and the intensity of their scrutiny. And the more explicit norms in the situation make behavioral expectations quite clear. Thereby, deviants can conform to the expected behavior and simulate belief. This is a chameleon-like or instrumental conformity that can usually pass muster in organizations and other impersonal situations. On the other hand, such simulation is much more difficult in small informal groups, where personal contact and scrutiny are closer and tend to be more intense and the norms and criteria of behavior are less explicit. Behavioral expectations often implicitly refer to a diffuse range of contexts, which are broader than in the formal situation. Insofar as membership tends to be voluntary and less instrumental, there is less incentive to dissimulate. If the group loses its attractiveness to trainees, motivation suffers and the pressure to remain in the situation

---

52. Irving Rosow, "Forms and Functions of Adult Socialization," *Social Forces*, 44 (1965) 35–45.

declines.[53] Hence, there is a constant screening process in informal settings which serves not only to control, but to attract and hold persons who genuinely share values—the more fully socialized members—and to exclude or estrange deviants whose hearts are not in it. Thereby, informal voluntary groups may display higher consensus and fuller socialization of trainees, while formal settings allow concealed deviants considerably more latitude for simulation and instrumental conformity.

In summary, of these factors that distinguish between formal and informal situations, fewer than one-half would tend to be conducive to the socialization of older persons. And these are largely correlates of small group size, in which any possible socialization processes would probably be concentrated. These include the generally high dependence of the elderly on those small groups to which they do belong, the likelihood of group support, the relative correspondence between ideal and real standards, and the limited prospect of successful concealment of deviant beliefs and behavior.

SOCIALIZATION TYPOLOGIES: FORMALITY AND STATUS CHANGE

Socialization to old age poses a special problem. It not only involves systematic status losses, but also, except for old-age institutions, the role transition takes place mainly in informal situations. These two variables delineate a four-fold typology that locates aging in a category of special cases: *informal socialization to a devalued position.* Incentives are weak and socialization mechanisms are less structured than in formal training situations. Consequently, indoctrination

---

53. This in no sense precludes the fact that groups may oppressively control or even tyrannize some members. But this is likely to be a short-run phenomenon and too instable a condition for long-term cohesion in free, genuinely voluntary groups whose members have other options.

promises to be less effective and socialization less definitive than under more favorable conditions. This may be evident from Figure 1, which shows different types of situations according to the patterning of status gain and formality of "training." Typical roles illustrate each pattern, and we can consider the various cells in turn.

Figure 1. TYPES OF SOCIALIZATION SITUATIONS

Status Change	Institutional Setting	
	Formal	Informal
Gain	Law School (Lawyer) West Point (Officer)	Family (Spouse) Social Elites
Loss	Prison (Convict) Mental Hospital (Patient)	(Illegitimate Mother) (Divorcee) (Old Person)

Formal Gain

Formal situations of status gain include the sharpest protypes of socialization. They represent training programs whose objectives include the indoctrination of attitudes as well as the transmission of knowledge and skill. While this type includes virtually all professional education, it also embraces instances as far-flung as upper-middle and upper class "finishing schools." It has not only the sharpest delineation of the situation and process, but also the most explicit goals and consciousness of purpose. Although the training content and values may vary, almost all formal socialization settings contain reasonably clear norms about a definite set of identifiable problems.

Formal Loss

By the same token, formal socialization to status loss also differentiates the socialization field rather sharply and has reasonably definite standards of commitment and behavior to be internalized. Control is prominent, rewards and punishments are used, and there is a greater reliance on discipline (punishment) than on incentives (reward) to secure conformity. One would expect such differences between the two formal situations because those involving gains prepare people for valued, often central, social roles, while those involving losses are oriented to various deviants. The typical social response to deviance is the imposition of control in order to limit disequilibrium and to affirm the legitimacy of violated values.[54]

Informal Gain

Informal situations of status gain include the socialization to many diverse roles. These may range from different valued group memberships to the most central roles in the society, such as family position. Recruits to existing statuses are informally indoctrinated with group expectations and values. Within different segments of society, such as social classes, this instruction, though informal, is institutionalized and displays striking regularities.[55] These situations may differ from formal settings in explicitness of structure and

54. Emile Durkheim, *The Division of Labor in Society* (Glencoe: Free Press, 1947).

55. Robert Sears, Eleanore Maccoby and Harry Levin, *Patterns of Child Rearing* (Evanston: Row, Peterson, 1957).

normative expectations. Occasionally, either the structure or the norms may be as explicit and sharp as in formal training, but it is uncommon for *both* to approximate formal settings in these respects.

Informal Loss

On the other hand, informal status losses usually differ from formal settings on both grounds. Even though deviance may be powerfully sanctioned (as traditionally in the case of illegitimate motherhood), learning a devalued new role usually occurs in a completely amorphous and unstructured situation. Norms appropriate to the position are typically vague and indefinite. Hence, such informal pressures as gossip and censure are neither integrated with nor reinforce an indoctrination process; nor are definite expectations and norms imposed as clear guides for the trainee's orientation. Not only is he often unable to "undo" or atone for his deviance, but usually he has little or no indication of how he is expected to behave either in the present or the future. This merely sustains the ambiguity of his situation and provides few clues for his adjustment or his social redemption.

This simply emphasizes the fact that there are few social definitions for the rehabilitation of certain classes of sin, deviance, and status loss. But it does not follow that all deviants are eternally damned by their society.[56] On the contrary, rehabilitation may be institutionalized, as in the prototype of confessions or self-denunciations in highly orthodox ideologies or authoritarian regimes, whether religious (the Catholic Church) or political (the Soviet or Chinese

---

56. Historically, even the most excluded and lowliest groups, such as slaves, lepers, and other pariahs, had explicit expectations about their behavior and role relations, however unpleasant these were. But now, even extreme deviance, such as incest, miscegenation, or other violated taboos, when not criminal offenses, seldom entail any positive role prescriptions by the society.

Communists). In such systems, until a "sinner" confesses his iniquity and accepts its implications, he cuts himself off from possible grace and salvation. But the confession of his offense acknowledges his negative status and may re-open a pathway to redemption and to some rewards or gains.[57] Under the appropriate conditions, then, there may be some incentive to accept a negative status or devalued position if this is the only viable means to rehabilitation, social reintegration, or the attainment of other inaccessible ends. Although *mea culpa* may be no "Open, Sesame!" it can initiate an effective salvage operation.

But such a perspective contains few incentives for the acceptance of old age. This generally offers little hope of salvation, reward, redemption, rehabilitation, or social reintegration in the face of the negative values about age that older and younger Americans share. For most of the elderly, the *acceptance* of old age simply becomes a metaphorical form of social suicide.

THE DISTINCTIVE SOCIALIZATION PROBLEM

The foregoing analysis indicates that the transition to old age in America represents a special problem in adult socialization, one with an unusual configuration. Normal

---

57. Although all confessions place one in a negative position, this is not necessarily a path to salvation. Indeed, they may seal one's doom by irrevocably condemning the person. In a totalitarian regime, confession may make rehabilitation possible and stave off execution or other implacable fate. But other confessions invite precisely the utter, final condemnation. For example, in the notorious Soviet trials of the late 'thirties, as in Arthur Koestler's *Darkness at Noon*, confession invited the death sentence on a charge of treason, counter-revolution, revisionism, or, from the regime's point of view, equally meaningful euphemisms. (Even in the West, confessions to political or capital crimes without extenuating qualifications offer the condemned no basis of social recovery.) Ironically, some of the Soviet confessions may have exemplified cases of *altruistic* suicide wherein the accused sacrificed themselves to the ideals of the revolution in which they and professedly their accusers believed—a perverse consensus by victim and executioner on ends justifying means.

status passages typically involve several conditions: new, valued social positions with reasonably clear norms, role continuity and status gains that motivate people to be socialized, commonly in formal programs. But becoming old presents just the opposite pattern in all these respects, specifically: (1) a *devalued position* (2) with *ambiguous norms*, (3) *role discontinuity*, and (4) *status loss* (5) that mobilizes *low motivation* or resistance to possible socialization (6) whose processes would be set in *informal contexts*. Thereby, on each factor, aging reverses the optimal conditions of socialization and presents a theoretical polar case.

Even waiving the vital moral issues, can socialization to a negative role be effective under such circumstances? Are any potent socializing forces available for people in such a situation? Are there other latent pressures or incentives that have not been identified or mobilized?[58] Are there effective levers to stimulate identification with an invidious role? In terms of sheer socialization theory, what are the possible prospects for socializing people to an aged role, and what are the necessary conditions for their socialization? In accordance with our check on the weakness of norms, how does the situation of the elderly appear on other variables that normally facilitate socialization?

Unfortunately, in the absence of systematic studies of socialization to old age, these questions cannot yet be definitively answered. Only a few scattered monographs or fragmentary reports about other significant status losses appear in the literature.[59] While some are impressive on other grounds, none specifically analyses crucial socialization vari-

---

58. Melvin Tumin, "Rewards and Task-Orientations," *American Sociological Review*, 20 (1955) 419–23.

59. Harold Garfinkel, "Conditions of Successful Degradation Ceremonies," *American Journal of Sociology*, 61 (1956) 420–24; William Goode, *After Divorce*; Harold Wilensky and Hugh Edwards, "The Skidder: Ideological Adjustments of Downward Mobile Workers," *American Sociological Review*, 24 (1959) 215–31.

ables. Nor has any systematic theory about status loss yet been advanced. Furthermore, the various decrements of old age constitute a significant deprivation[60] relative both to the person's own past life and to that of younger contemporaries. This implies that earlier norms persist into old age.

At the same time, the youthful self-images of the elderly prove remarkably impervious to the different perceptions of them by significant others.[61] This is the only instance of this kind in the entire professional literature. Others' definitions of someone as old do not significantly affect his own view of himself, although self-conceptions are usually a function of others' perceptions. It has been suggested that persons whose self-images differ from others' views of them probably have multiple reference groups that disagree.[62] Thereby, their favorable self-conception can be anchored in and supported by *some* group. But this seems unlikely in the case of the old because of their patent denial of a social reality that others' views reflect. This in no way precludes their capitalizing on others' positive definitions if these should occur. But defensively ignoring or denying unfavorable perceptions is a form of social autism that cannot be conducive to socialization, for this basically involves the incorporation of social attitudes. Therefore, a successful transition to old age presumably *requires* a shift in the actor's reference groups as a source of norms about a new role for him.[63]

---

60. Robert Merton and Alice Rossi, "Contributions to the Theory of Reference Group Behavior," in Robert Merton and Paul Lazarsfeld (eds.), *Continuities in Social Research: Studies in the Scope and Method of "The American Soldier"* (Glencoe: Free Press, 1950) 40–105.

61. Zena Blau, "Changes in Status and Age Identification," *American Sociological Review*, 21 (1956) 198–203; Morton Deutsch and Leonard Solomon, "Reactions to Evaluations by Others as Influenced by Self-Evaluations," *Sociometry*, 22 (1959) 93–112.

62. Leo Reeder, George Donahue and Arturo Biblarz, "Conceptions of Self and Others," *American Journal of Sociology*, 66 (1960) 153–59.

63. Harold Kelley, *op. cit.*

7. *Socialization Structures and Old Age*

OUR ANALYSIS indicates that prevailing institutional forces and dominant values militate against the effective socialization of Americans to old age. At the same time, normal socialization structures are not sufficiently mobilized to counteract these forces. The cultural values provide feeble incentives to accept an aged role, while the informal situation of most of the elderly (notably those who have lost central adult roles) activates few compelling socializing mechanisms.

Significantly, the old have the same stereotypes and prejudices against other elderly people as the young, but they exempt themselves personally from such invidious judgments. They deny they are old and dissociate themselves from other aged. This signifies their continued commitment to the prevailing perspectives about aging despite significant changes in their own circumstances. To be sure, this involves a cognitive problem of self-images, but not one of *value change*, for the elderly deprecate old age just as younger people do. Formally stated, the old and young agree in their evaluation of a possible aged *status*, but not about its *incumbents*. Younger people perceive the aging as old; the elderly readily agree to this classification of *other* aged, but reject such a definition of themselves personally. The acceptance of old age and others' images of them inevitably hastens their alienation, without any compensating hope of social recovery.[1] Hence, the motives for embracing such social losses are understandably weak. The gross motivational forces are reasonably simple and clear.

Coupled with old people's reluctance, the available socializing forces also tend to be ineffective. An exhaustive, systematic analysis of socialization mechanisms is beyond the scope of this paper. But we can consider several of the more important socialization variables and relate them to aging. These concern not only authority and peer groups, but other factors normally conducive to socialization in earlier status transitions. This will complete our review of the situation of the elderly for the presence of common socialization variables.

OTHER VARIABLES NORMALLY FACILITATING SOCIALIZATION[2]

New Role Sets

Earlier status successions typically place the person in *new role sets* that pattern his relationships. This is seen, for

---

1. Irving Rosow, "Old Age: One Moral Dilemma of an Affluent Society," *Gerontologist*, 2 (1962) 182–91.
2. These factors are not only analyzed at length in Irving Rosow, "Situational Forces in Adult Socialization" (unpublished manuscript), but several of them are mentioned among the hypotheses on role adjustment set forth by Leonard Cottrell ("Adjustment of the Individual to his Age and Sex Roles," *American Sociological Review*, 7 [1942] 617–20). While socialization theory is only tangentially concerned with adjustment per se, this can readily be analyzed as a function of socialization variables when status changes are involved.

example, in his entry to the full-time labor force on the completion of his education. The role set structures expectations and embeds them in social ties that guide the person's behavior.[3] Moving into old age, however, seldom entails the transition into a new role set or even the retention of many established ones. On the contrary, the progressive loss of statuses results in the attrition of role sets. This is true both for central and secondary roles. For men, voluntary and involuntary retirement means removal from a work group, with no substitute for it. For men and women, widowhood is a critical disruption of the nuclear family set, although parental and grandparental relationships may be maintained. Widowhood probably has greater impact on the wife than on the husband, insofar as women's central roles are in the family. Participation in formal organizations also systematically declines, without the substitution of new memberships. And friendships inevitably dwindle, not only with the death or movement of friends, but also with role changes that are premature within the norms and experience of a group.[4] Zena Blau reports that newly widowed women tend to be excluded from their circles of married friends, and they have no viable substitutes for these lost relationships. Eventually some of these former friends may be recovered after a substantial portion of them—perhaps one-third to one-half—in turn become widowed.[5] Generally, then, aging is not a successive process of losing one role set and acquiring another

---

3. Robert Merton, "The Role Set: Problems in Sociological Theory," *British Journal of Sociology*, 8 (1957) 106–20, and *Social Theory and Social Structure*, rev. ed. (Glencoe: Free Press, 1957) 368–84.

4. Zena Blau, "Structural Constraints on Friendships in Old Age," *American Sociological Review*, 26 (1961) 429–39; David Riesman, "Some Clinical and Cultural Aspects of Aging," *American Journal of Sociology*, 59 (1954) 379–83. For an excellent study of normatively early and late role change, see Corinne Nydegger, "Timing of Fatherhood: Role Perception and Socialization" (Unpub. Ph.D. Thesis, Penn State University, 1973).

5. Zena Blau, *op. cit.*

to replace it as in earlier status successions. This incipient socializing mechanism does not function.

The shrinking role sets and role ambiguity together remove older people from a major socialization pressure. A role set not only establishes expectations, but also functions to assure conformity and limit deviance from these standards. All its members have a stake in the norms that govern relations within the set.[6] Thus, in any transaction, the interested parties are not only ego and alter, but also *third parties* who exert pressure on alter to exact correct behavior from ego. This controls deviance, maintains the system, and stabilizes its norms. Examples of this abound in the sociological literature, but the principle is sharpened when spontaneously expressed in more exotic contexts. An excellent illustration that appears in classic scholarship deals with the administration of justice within the aristocratic *genos* (clan) in Homeric Greece:[7]

> Observe also that the king was not free to refrain from proceeding against one of his own sons, for example, if the latter were involved. Thus, the hero Tydeus had killed his cousins in defending his father Oeneus, and the latter had neglected to punish the crime. Oeneus' brother, Agrios, then intervened along with his family, forced Tydeus to flee and Oeneus to abdicate. Which shows how a denial of justice might lead to the dethronement of the king-judge.

---

6. Various sociologists, especially Goode, have focused attention on the interests of third parties in social transactions and the factors that govern how their interests vary (William Goode, "Norm Commitment and Conformity to Role-Status Obligations," *American Journal of Sociology*, 66 [1960] 246–58, and "A Theory of Role Strain," *American Sociological Review*, 25 [1960] 483–96). Also cf. Peter Blau, *Exchange and Power in Social Life* (New York: John Wiley, 1964); Albert Cohen, "The Sociology of the Deviant Act: Anomie Theory and Beyond," *American Sociological Review*, 30 (1965) 5–14; and Richard Emerson, "Power-Dependence Relations," *American Sociological Review*, 27 (1962) 31–41.

7. Emile Mireaux, *Daily Life in the Time of Homer* (New York: Macmillan, 1959).

Thus, principals are not simply free to adjudicate their relations directly; others also have a major stake in the principles that govern those relations and will protect this by enforcing stable role obligations and norms. However, as older people lose role sets, there are few pressures on them to observe many norms, for few people have any stake in their conformity—beyond their incipient dependency and thereby the maintenance of their self-sufficiency and health.

Rites of Passage

Second, socialization is usually facilitated by a formal, explicit status change, one clearly marked in time and observed by ceremonies of initiation, graduation, or a similar *rite de passage*. The symbols of status transition redefine the person socially and publicly signify the change in norms and behavior suitable to his new position. But, as we have seen, the dividing line between middle age and old age is amorphous and indistinct. The specific transition itself seldom corresponds to any particular social stigma, nor is it sharply punctuated by definite events, ritualistic or otherwise. Aging is a steady, but gradual process, creeping along with subtle changes, few of them dramatic and none of them fully decisive. And, as has been indicated earlier, the *social* redefinition of a person as old usually precedes rather than follows such specific events as retirement and widowhood.

Isolation from Former Groups

Third, during transition to a new role, socialization is fostered by a trainee's *isolation from his former group memberships* and supports. This maximizes his dependence upon the new socializing group and increases the situational pressures for his conformity to its standards. Conversely, the supports of competing reference groups are minimized and the norms of the socializing group strengthened. For this reason, many training programs intentionally isolate recruits, such as army inductees, novices in religious orders, and even patients in sanatoria.[8]

Aging, however, does not abruptly wrench a person from all his previous groups at one fell swoop. Rather, memberships and group supports gradually dwindle away. While isolation and loneliness often do develop, they result from a process that allows the person to adjust continually to his changing circumstances. This does not mean that this loss of social contacts occasions an older person's enthusiasm. But these losses are gradual and tend to be incomplete. Most relatively isolated persons manage to retain some threads, however tenuous, of social contact.[9] While group memberships suffer drastic attrition in the later years, people are not utterly cut off from all previous associates. The heart of the aging process is that this reduction is gradual though steady, allowing some ongoing adjustment. But the crucial factor is that the loss of former groups is not compensated by the acquisition of new ones.

There is evidence that status successions are intrinsically disruptive,[10] and rituals such as honeymoons or other mechanisms which isolate novices from their former groups may facilitate the transition to a new status. Such isolation

8. Bruno Bettelheim reports that the separation from and break in communication with family, friends, and other former associates were instrumental in breaking the resistance of new concentration camp prisoners, forcing their acceptance of the camp as their world and alienating them from their intimates outside (Bruno Bettelheim, "Individual and Mass Behavior in Extreme Situations," *Journal of Abnormal and Social Psychology*, 38 [1943] 417–52.)

9. For an interesting analysis of the functions of confidants, see Marjorie Lowenthal, *Lives in Distress* (New York: Basic Books, 1964).

10. Robert Ellis and W. Clayton Lane, "Social Mobility and Social Isolation: A Test of Sorokin's Dissociative Hypothesis," *American Sociological Review*, 32 (1967) 237–53.

is most common in formal institutional settings. But when it is not used, there is often a functional substitute for it, even in informal situations. This is the mechanism that Rose Coser has called "role distance."[11] She indicates:

> In learning new roles, a person . . . faces different expectations from various reference groups who all have an interest in his growth, yet who define his growth in different ways; at the same time, each reference group expects him to live up to role requirements surrounding his present as well as his future status.
>
> Different role partners interested in a person's growth, though all expecting signs of abandonment of the earlier status, often differ in their prescriptions or preferences as to the manner in which this is done.

In status successions, role distance is simply "distancing," or the process of withdrawal from an earlier role and its associates when acquiring a new one.[12] It is a form of social molting. When a person faces conflicting expectations between members of the old and new role sets, abandoning the earlier status becomes a mechanism of socialization. It weakens counterinfluences and strengthens identification with the new position and its norms. One study of medical residents exemplifies this process in their change of standards. With greater experience, their professional competence and commitment to differences in medical status increased, and their attitudes toward superiors and subordinates correspondingly changed. Consequently, the residents became more equalitarian in relation to other physicians, but more distant from nurses.[13] Hence, their movement indicated an aspect of role

---

11. Rose Coser, "Role Distance, Sociological Ambivalence, and Transitional Status Systems," *American Journal of Sociology*, 72 (1966) 173–87.

12. Coser's use of "role distance" differs from that of Erving Goffman.

13. Melvin Seeman and John Evans, "Apprenticeship and Attitude Change," *American Journal of Sociology*, 67 (1962) 365–78.

distancing—withdrawal from those of lower status as they established their qualification for a new superior status. Similarly, in any role distance, nonconformity with old standards means a broken identification; conformity with new expectations signifies an identification with new norms. Thus, role distance helps to anticipate and resolve possible role conflicts by articulating a clear choice of one reference group over another. Although it is not particularly salient in the case of the aged, this process is intensified when the actor functions in a position of high visibility.[14]

The first three factors—new role sets, *rites of passage,* and isolation from former groups—highlight the importance of *two* clear positions in any status succession. The earlier and later positions are the equivalent of *before* and *after* stages in any process. And this underscores a major dilemma in the socialization to old age. The mechanisms of socialization normally operate to loosen or destroy old group ties while offering rewarding new ones in their stead. And the transition to new positions is facilitated by role clarity and the rewards that stimulate motivation. But the aged have few incentives and encounter normative ambiguity. Lost responsibilities and capacities reduce expectations others have of them. Their loss of former positions and role sets is not balanced by new statuses and groups to which they succeed. Therefore, the old tend to cling to their former middle-age identity, often more rigidly than, in an opposite case, socially mobile persons reject their social origins.[15] While they have a given point of origin in prospective socialization (before), they have no future group and position that can compensate for their social losses (after). Thus, in the transition to old age, the amorphous socialization objectives and the dearth

---

14. Rose Coser, "Insulation from Observability and Types of Social Conformity," *American Sociological Review*, 25 (1961) 28–39.

15. Robert Ellis and W. Clayton Lane, "Social Mobility and Career Orientation," *Sociology and Social Research*, 50 (1966) 280–95.

of new groups simply emphasize the absence of that social growth and acquisition which typify most earlier status successions.

Ignoring Other Status Differences

Fourth, socialization is almost invariably fostered by *disregarding recruits' other status differences,* both past and present, and emphasizing their similarity within the training arena. This is achieved by the "homogenization" of entering trainees and by stressing the common situation, problems, and fate they currently share. This vitalizes the peer group and minimizes the influence of previous status advantages on current position and prospects, thereby shifting the orientation of trainees from external to internal reference groups. Whenever uniforms and standard dress are issued to recruits —as in police, military, medical, or religious training—this is an overt means of "levelling" trainees. By disrupting former status differences and standardizing beginning statuses, a discontinuity is introduced that is functional for socialization. This is not to say that any stratification of the peer group is disfunctional; it speaks only of stratification based on external criteria.

In old age, the relation between previous and current statuses shows several patterns. The most common is the effort to preserve the status characteristics of middle age, including roles, self-images and class advantages. The second is a rear-guard delaying action against social and personal losses which threaten the individual's life pattern. These include major role attrition in widowhood and retirement and their correlates of failing health and reduced income. They often entail the sacrifice of customary living standards and even the loss of prestige in downward social mobility. This pattern may allow a reluctant private acknowledgment, but still a public denial, of objective losses.[16] Sacrifices are concealed, and a facade of little change is erected, one relieved of close scrutiny through social withdrawal. By and large, the strains of pretense are not resolved, and the differences between past and present status characteristics are at best only awkwardly accommodated in a doomed holding action. The third pattern actually does minimize previous social differences and emphasizes current similarities. It is commonly reported for many retirement centers in Florida, the Southwest, and the Pacific coast, where the previous life styles of many migrants change, often adumbrating former social differences. To be sure, some special centers, such as Moosehaven and Salhaven in Florida, specifically recruit people of similar occupation and background. But such a homogeneous population begs the question of the function of preretirement social distinctions. Other retirement centers presumably draw on more diverse groups, whose background differences are reputedly subordinated to their similarities in the organization of social life.[17] But, typically, these self-selected middle-class people have only nominal status differences, which are of minor importance for the present problem.

In social mobility, both background and current position are usually reflected in later attitudes. That is, people who are mobile express attitudes intermediate to those of

---

16. Irving Rosow, *Social Integration of the Aged* (New York: Free Press, 1967) 278–85.

17. Gordon Aldridge, "Informal Social Relationships in a Retirement Community," *Marriage and Family Living*, 21 (1959) 70–72; Ernest Burgess (ed.), *Retirement Villages* (Ann Arbor: University of Michigan, Division of Gerontology, 1961), and Ernest Burgess, "Social Relations, Activities and Personal Adjustment," *American Journal of Sociology*, 59 (1954) 352–60; G.C. Hoyt, "The Life of the Retired in a Trailer Park," *American Journal of Sociology*, 59 (1954) 361–70; L.C. Michelon, "The New Leisure Class," *American Journal of Sociology*, 59 (1954) 371–78.

the two strata they have spanned.[18] But as to the *relative* strengths of past vs. present positions, one's background seems to have less force than the current situation.[19] This clearly applies to the nouveau riche and to the sharp Republican switch of the new suburbanites in the 1952 Presidential election. Also, in determining both attitudes and behavior among the problematic ethnic minorities in the Soviet Union, contemporary social class position was far more potent than traditionally divisive national allegiances.[20] Certainly people's behavior is predicted better by their current objective circumstances than by their initial attitudes,[21] especially when technical competence becomes a relevant factor.[22] This simply generalizes the underlying premise of dissonance theory.[23] In other words, the constraints of reality pressures are significant and compelling, and their strength in relation to established patterns cannot be casually dismissed—even if they are not uniformly binding. In this vein, Blau also reports that occupational prestige ratings are not significantly affected by respondents' social mobility, nor by the direction of that mobility.[24] Yet the unimportance of directionality seems to be an extreme conclusion. It is doubtful that downward mobility has quite the same effect as upward mobility. People's most advantaged position is probably weighted. Therefore, later status is probably less determinate of atti-

---

18. Peter Blau, "Social Mobility and Interpersonal Relations," *American Sociological Review*, 21 (1956) 290–95; Alex Inkeles and Raymond Bauer, *The Soviet Citizen* (Cambridge: Harvard University Press, 1959).

19. Alex Inkeles and Raymond Bauer, *op. cit.*

20. *Ibid.*

21. Seymour Bellin and Louis Kriesberg, "Relationship Among Attitudes, Circumstances, and Behavior: The Case of Applying for Public Housing," *Sociology and Social Research*, 51 (1967) 453–69.

22. Ralph Underhill, "Values and Post-College Career Change," *American Journal of Sociology*, 72 (1966) 163–72.

23. Natalie and Alphonse Chapanis, "Cognitive Dissonance: Five Years Later," *Psychological Bulletin*, 61 (1964) 1–22.

24. Peter Blau, "Occupational Bias and Mobility," *American Sociological Review*, 22 (1957) 392–99.

tudes than former status only *after* downward mobility. Indeed, Wilensky and Edwards report that downward occupational mobility intensifies previous value commitments and makes workers even more conservative than those in their terminal class.[25] In other words, the status-deprived tend to deny failure and strive for success, asserting and reinforcing the values of their former position, i.e., those that nominally confer the greatest advantage.

Accordingly, by this principle, older people generally emphasize and value their former status rather than deprecate it. They try to sustain and maximize those earlier status advantages that their current situation does not grossly undermine and repudiate. This principally takes the form of dissociating themselves (privately and publicly) from current losses and symbolically asserting the continuity of earlier life stages. This is the meaning of old people's *denial* of their actual or impending old age and of their reactions to status deprivation. Thus, they minimize their objective losses in order to deny or mitigate the social consequences.

New Conformity Criteria

Fifth, socialization pressures are intensified by *reducing rewards for conformity to previous norms and increasing rewards for meeting new norms.*[26] This represents a weaning from one role to another or, in learning theory, the extinction of one set of responses and the conditioning of another. The conception of appropriate behavior is shifted and new expectations are established through reinforcement. This is, of course, a cardinal principle in all socialization.

---

25. Harold Wilensky and Hugh Edwards, "The Skidder: Ideological Adjustments of Downward Mobile Workers," *American Sociological Review*, 24 (1959) 215–31.

26. Harry Bredemeier and Richard Stephenson, *The Analysis of Social Systems* (New York: Holt, Rinehart and Winston, 1962).

However, its effectiveness requires systematic application which is virtually precluded in the typical aging process.
People's conformity to adult norms continues to gratify and
be rewarded throughout middle age. Maintaining independence is rewarded, not penalized. The fifties are a transition
period when such rewards slow down. Earning levels normally rise during adult working years to reach a peak in the
late forties, levelling off or gradually declining in the fifties.
It is most unusual for salary *growth rates* to be sustained
through the sixth decade, and they almost invariably decline
after age sixty. Hence, the rewards for continuing to observe
earlier norms do fall off, but this sets in gradually rather than
abruptly and does not clearly make previous standards obsolete or inappropriate for the aging person. On the contrary,
the norms themselves are not depreciated; what is depreciated
is their relevance to the older person and implicitly, his ability
to continue to meet them. To the extent that he does meet
them, his rewards may continue, even if at reduced levels.
But they certainly decline if he fails to meet them. This is
attended by the shift of the older person from an achieved
to an ascribed status. He comes to be judged by age rather
than by performance criteria. Accordingly, it is *not* that conformity is rewarded, but that *nonconformity* is penalized.[27]
This failure is the converse of the earlier pattern in which
previous norms are outgrown and new ones acquired, the
basic condition of most status successions. Furthermore, the
loss of former rewards is not complemented by increased rewards for meeting new sets of standards. The lack of new
expectations and the flexibility of possible new role definitions would alone preclude this. They indicate the dearth of
norms by which conformity can be judged and rewards dis-

---

27. Theodore Sarbin, "Notes on the Transformation of Social Identity," in L. M. Roberts, N. S. Greenfield and M. H. Miller (eds.), *Comprehensive Mental Health* (Madison: University of Wisconsin Press, 1968)
97–115.

tributed. New conformity patterns have few significant functions for the social system, either in helping to maintain it or in avoiding systemic strains. Hence, there is little stake or investment in new norms for the aged, and, as a result, there are neither new standards nor systematic rewards for their observance.

Role Clarity

Sixth, socialization is also fostered by *role clarity,* which assists in the cognitive aspect of learning. The more clearly a role can be defined and described, the more readily can a trainee grasp its content and the norms and expectations by which it is governed. Even though he has yet to master the necessary skills, he can at least understand what he must learn, what is expected of him, what his responsibilities and prerogatives are. Such specification is epitomized in formal job descriptions (in their stodgiest form, in Civil Service Bulletins). Implicit in role clarity is specificity.

However, the steadily declining responsibilities of old age reduce positive role prescriptions for older people. There are fewer and fewer things that they are either required or expected to do. Indeed, the role actually loses structure and becomes vague, ambiguous, amorphous. Insofar as few people depend on the aged or are affected by their action and decisions, the scope for their individual preference and choice grows. The role is most diffuse and subject to a broad range of personal options that indicate how limited are others' expectations of the elderly. There are few general principles that integrate a conception of their proper behavior. And those definite norms about which there is considerable agreement tend to be *pro*scriptions that specify what is disapproved. For example, as our earlier review showed, presumably older people should not relinquish social contacts, should not marry somebody very much younger than themselves,

should not go on relief if it can possibly be avoided, etc.[28] On
the whole, these are proscriptions against deviance, such as
may be found with other roles. But they are not balanced by
a corresponding set of *pre*scriptions about what is required
or expected. Hence, old people must largely create their own
private role definitions, for the culture does not provide
these clearly.[29]

Role Rehearsal

Seventh, *the opportunity to rehearse future roles* is one
of the major levers of socialization. This gives the role a
reality in experience which lends it depth and promotes identification. By rehearsing a real role or its facsimile, direct
experience concretizes it. This involves the difference between *Wissen* and *Koennen*; experience transcends both the
abstractness of knowledge alone and the vagueness or illusion
of imagination. While readily apparent in learning such kin-
esthetic skills as swimming, dancing, or driving a car, it is
equally relevant to subtler experiences, as in learning to
make love. These cannot be mastered passively, but only
with practice. Thus, rehearsal confers insight and a grasp of
interaction and relationships which knowledge without experience can at best only superficially approximate. For this
reason, supervised clinical training is central to most professional curricula, such as medicine, social work, dentistry,
and teaching. Obviously, in aging there are no patterned opportunities to rehearse future roles directly. Not simply because the role is so devalued that there is little incentive, but
rather because it is so diffuse and indefinite. Without clear
expectations, there is no significant opportunity to rehearse

---

28. Robert Havighurst, "Flexibility and the Social Roles of the
Retired," *American Journal of Sociology*, 59 (1954) 309–11; Robert
Havighurst and Ruth Albrecht, *Older People* (New York: Longmans &
Green, 1953).

29. Cf. William Goode, *After Divorce* (Glencoe: Free Press 1956).

a future role. It would be difficult to tell an aging person precisely what and how to rehearse.[30] Lipman's data reflect the limited value of the "empty nest" stage for the rehearsal of retirement roles.[31]

Rehearsal also typically exposes the trainee to other members of his prospective role set. Indeed, it is probably impossible to learn a role meaningfully except through interaction with a definite role set. Not only are the norms themselves concretized, but the potential strains from conflicting expectations are experienced in a more pervasive fashion than is possible when the standards are simply learned intellectually, and not applied. Thereby, practice becomes a trial run for role-playing. With the amorphousness of aged norms and the haphazard variation in role sets, the lack of rehearsal limits any identification that otherwise might develop with a future role.

Committing Activity

Eighth, rehearsal is one specialized form of *activity* which cultivates skills, techniques and insight into the role. Such activity in all its forms has two vital socializing effects: (a) it tends to increase a trainee's ego investment in and commitment to the status, and (b) it changes his self-images in a manner appropriate to the role.[32] It can achieve these even

30. This is an a priori limiting factor in the potential success of preretirement counseling programs. While the ambitious ones advocate a youthful ideal role, this is not systematically supported by objective life conditions nor by the definitions of other reference groups or the culture. Indeed, counsels of youthfulness actually project ideals of deviant behavior vis-a-vis general cultural stereotypes.

31. Aaron Lipman, "Role Conceptions and Morale of Couples in Retirement," *Journal of Gerontology*, 16 (1961) 267–71.

32. Howard Becker and James Carper, "The Development of Identification with an Occupation," *American Journal of Sociology*, 61 (1956) 289–98, and "The Elements of Identification with an Occupation," *American Sociological Review*, 21 (1956) 341–48; Robert Merton, George Reader and Patricia Kendall, *The Student-Physician* (Cambridge: Harvard University Press, 1957).

in the face of his initial reservations or resistance.[33] However, there are no special skills or activities peculiar to old age whose mastery can intensify ego investments in growing old.

Other Committing Forces

Ninth, role transitions and socialization are normally facilitated by other *forces of commitment*. Among the more important in a longer series are such variables as: positive aspiration to the role; voluntary participation in socialization; continuity of roles in a status sequence; anticipatory socialization in advance of training or practice; trainees constituting a visible, viable social group rather than simply a social category; trainee competition for scarce awards based on superior performance; the command of adaptive skills; a fixed or finite period of training rather than an interminable or open-ended one; the freedom of training from gratuitous cross-role conflicts; and the absence of alternative roles as possible substitutes for the training goals.[34]

Such conditions are uniformly and independently conducive to socialization. Yet, aside from the freedom from role conflicts, the possible preparation for old age does not effectively mobilize these variables as committing forces. The aging normally do not want to be old, their voluntary participation in socializing activity is extremely low,[35] there is little

33. Leon Festinger, *A Theory of Cognitive Dissonance* (Evanston: Row, Peterson, 1957).

34. Irving Rosow, "Situational Forces in Adult Socialization."

35. Their participation rates in special activities such as Golden Age clubs seldom exceed 3 percent (Joseph Downing, "Factors Affecting the Selective Use of a Social Club for the Aged," *Journal of Gerontology*, 12 [1957] 81–84; Bernard Kutner, *et al.*, *Five Hundred Over Sixty* [New York: Russell Sage, 1956]; *The States and their Older Citizens* [Chicago: Council of State Governments, 1955]) except in isolated instances (Peter Townsend, *Family Life of Old People* [London: Routledge & Kegan Paul, 1957]) or under special conditions which integrate these programs with retirement housing settings (Ernest Burgess, "Social Relations, Activities and Personal Adjustment;" Irving Rosow, "Retirement Housing and So-

role continuity and virtually no anticipatory socialization, they represent a social category more than distinctive groups, there is no indoctrination, there are no competitive performance tests and few distinctive adaptive skills, there is no fixed training period, and many optional role definitions are possible. Minimizing or denying age is the dominant substitute for an older self-image.

Successful Performance

Tenth, *successful role performance* normally facilitates socialization. But in old age there is little basis of "successful" performance except in non-aged terms, even in retirement communities that usually place a premium on the maintenance of youthfulness. We will presently consider the implications of this in connection with the possible genesis of local norms and older role models.

AUTHORITY FIGURES:
ROLE REVERSAL AND ROLE MODELS[36]

The conditions of socialization to old age differ significantly from those of earlier periods, and nowhere is this clearer than in the trainees' relations to authority figures. Actually, for the aged there is no functional equivalent of an authority group—either normatively or as a source of role models—except in patterns inimical to socialization. There may of course be real authority figures over them, especially as older people become increasingly dependent or senile. But

---

cial Integration, *Gerontologist*, 1 [1961] 85–91, also in Clark Tibbitts and Wilma Donahue [eds.], *Social and Psychological Aspects of Aging* [New York: Columbia University Press, 1962] 327–40; Irving Webber, "The Organized Social Life of the Retired: Two Florida Communities," *American Journal of Sociology*, 59 [1954] 340–45).

36. This analysis applies only to the aged living in the community, not to the 3 percent living in institutions. The two contexts pose totally different socialization situations and problems.

this only hardens the general pattern of **role reversal,** in which those with superior power and authority are almost invariably younger persons—adult children or relatives, various professionals (doctors, social workers, clergy, etc.) or other middle-aged groups. This role reversal has become axiomatic in terms of potential role models of the aged, for their admired models tend to be younger persons who personify the competence that the old themselves had in the past.[37] In the course of their adult lives the aged have normally been in authority over those younger than themselves, but seldom have they been subordinate to them. Thus, when they become subordinate to younger persons, the customary intergenerational roles are reversed. Superior responsibility, power, and often competence then reside in the younger rather than the older group. There is absolutely no systematic precedent for this in the life experience of the aged.[38] Indeed the very fact of their inferior position testifies not only to their waning independence, but also to their declining social competence and autonomy. Old age displays no social growth that typifies earlier status successions, but only inevitable and presumably irreversible social decline.

An incisive prototype of such role reversal is illustrated in a report on the operations of private employment agencies that have recently burgeoned to service the demand for professional and white collar employees. As labor market brokers, agency personnel view job applicants as commodities to be processed for easy placement, commonly in prospective positions for which they will be overqualified and/or underpaid. Job counselors adopt the tactic of "conditioning the applicant," subtly humiliating him by systematic depreciation of his market value and the undermining of his self-esteem.

---

37. Raymond Payne, "Some Theoretical Approaches to the Sociology of Aging," *Social Forces,* 38 (1960) 359–62.
38. Harold Orbach and David Shaw, "Social Participation and the Role of the Aging," *Geriatrics,* 12 (1957) 241–46.

The purpose is to soften up the client, lower his aspirations, reduce his demands and expectations, and thereby make it easier to place him in a job. Because of the tremendous growth of such agencies in recent years, most counselors are fairly young, many of them in their twenties. For our present purposes, the crucial encounter confronts an older professional applicant with a young job counselor:[39]

> The age of the counselors is another factor in controlling applicants, especially older, professionally-trained ones. Many of these applicants, in fact, seem to feel the need of a kind of Freudian fatherfigure; and they are uncomfortable with counselors much younger than they are.
>
> In several cases, for example, job-seekers called the agency in response to newspaper ads. Over the telephone, they seemed eager to find out what was available. The counselor, age 22, made appointments with them to come to the agency.
>
> Soon after meeting with their counselor, who was fairly successful in conditioning applicants, the applicants' attitude changed from one of ready cooperation to reservation —a reverse conditioning. In each case, the job-seekers were more than 20 years older than the counselor. The applicants probably felt that the younger man was incapable of advising them in an important decision. In these cases, applicant control was impossible. (Sometimes the manager would perceive this and keep older applicants away from younger counselors.)

Though such applicants are seldom of retirement age, they still experience a definite reversal of intergenerational power that places them in an inferior position. The dependence symbolized by such role reversal is both a stage and reflection of their denouement, and it seldom arouses any enthusiasm in the "mature" client. The reactions to such role

---

39. Thomas Martinez, "Why Employment-Agency Counselors Lower Their Clients' Self-Esteem," *Trans-Action*, 5 (March, 1968) 20–25.

reversal are quite familiar to social workers, physicians, adult children, and others who assume responsibility for the dependent older person. They often find the aged irrational, irascible, capricious, and stubborn over apparent trivialities, without recognizing the signs of a desperate rearguard action to retain vestiges of the dignity, control, and independence that are steadily slipping away.

Furthermore, those in authority over the aged can have little value as **potential role models** for them. They have no personal experience as older people themselves and therefore cannot be role models comparable to teachers in professional training. Under optimal conditions, they might conceivably be coaches in the manner of male obstetricians with their patients. That is, they might possibly be a source of counsel or guidance, but not personal models for direct emulation. Indeed, as potential aged role models, they really personify replicas of the older person's own *past*. Not experienced exemplars on which to base his future development, they represent states that he had achieved earlier and which he has lost or is currently in the process of losing. Hence, as possible role models, younger authorities and reference figures can only symbolize the old person's competent past rather than a future which portends his waning capacities. Yet he needs no external models for these earlier life stages. For if the approximation of a past younger state is the ideal, then he is fairly self-sufficient and can be his own model. His problem is not to fashion an image of a youthful goal and then to give that image form and substance, but rather to halt his decline from that former state. Consequently, while younger authorities may exercise power over the old through control and reward, this power does not rest on their experience and special competence as models for an aged role.

Hence, for older people the models of youthful authority are gratuitous. The problem as they see it lies not in their faulty conception of an adequate adult role, but simply in their ability to preserve it. And here either the spirit is willing and the flesh weak, or the person is able but the social system unyielding. Therefore, even the middle aged cannot function as effective older role models in any sense comparable to seasoned authority figures in other socialization contexts.

THE PEER GROUP

It is axiomatic that one of the basic functions of the peer group is to provide support for its members. This may be as true of competitive socialization situations as of informal expressive groups.[40] Evan, for example, reports on an engineering company that split up and assigned its trainees to various departments singly, in pairs, and in groups of three or more.[41] Those assigned in the larger groups remained with the company after their training was over significantly more often than those trained alone or in pairs. This reflected differences in peer support with which trainees could meet the strains and demands of their indoctrination. Group support is important not only for conventional groups, but for deviants as well, both in promoting socialization[42] and in stiffening members' resistance to authorities' socialization pressures.[43] Indeed, group support helps members to conform, even though

40. Irving Rosow, "Situational Forces in Adult Socialization."

41. William Evan, "Peer-Group Interaction and Organizational Socialization," *American Sociological Review*, 28 (1963) 436–40.

42. LaMar Empey and Jerome Rabow, "The Provo Experiment in Delinquency Rehabilitation," *American Sociological Review*, 26 (1961) 679–95; Robert and Rhona Rapoport and Irving Rosow, *Community as Doctor* (London: Tavistock, 1960).

43. Peter Garabedian, "Social Roles and Processes of Socialization in the Prison Community," *Social Problems*, 11 (Fall, 1963) 139–52; George Grosser, "The Role of Informal Inmate Groups in Change of Values," *Children*, 5 (1958) 25–29; Warren Roland, "Cultural, Personal and Situational Roles," *Sociology and Social Research*, 34 (September–October, 1949) 104–11; Stanton Wheeler, "Socialization in Correctional Communities," *American Sociological Review*, 26 (1961) 697–712; Ronald Wulbert, "Inmate Pride in Total Institutions," *American Journal of Sociology*, 71 (1965) 1–9.

a characteristic pattern has been noted of incipient defection from group values as the time approaches for some to leave the group through graduation or release from institutions.[44] In general, group support raises morale[45] and is crucial in integrating members and assisting them in meeting various crises.

In contrast, except for a minority who prefer solitude, the isolated trainee who has no significant social ties generally tends to become demoralized. For example, solitary workers who have no social contact with their fellows tend to be significantly more alienated than those who work together or at least see each other outside.[46] Demoralization is a common response to isolation in later life, especially when this is a new experience, a change from previous patterns which is linked with role losses.[47] Thus, isolation and the breakdown of group supports are most consequential when they are involuntary and represent a sharp change from the life style of middle age.[48]

But, just as there is no viable authority group for the socialization of old people, there is at best only a most amorphous peer group. Although older people have some visibility, this is not reinforced by strong age groupings that pro-

---

44. Howard Becker and Blanche Geer, "The Fate of Idealism in Medical School," *American Sociological Review*, 23 (1958) 50–56; Stanton Wheeler, *op. cit.*

45. Robert Davis, "The Relationship of Social Preferability to Self-Concept in an Aged Population," *Journal of Gerontology*, 17 (1962) 431–36; Derek Phillips, "Social Participation and Happiness," *American Journal of Sociology*, 72 (1967) 479–88.

46. Leonard Pearlin, "Alienation from Work," *American Sociological Review*, 27 (1962) 314–26.

47. Marjorie Lowenthal, "Social Isolation and Mental Illness in Old Age," *American Sociological Review*, 29 (1964) 54–70; Marjorie Lowenthal and Deetje Boler, "Voluntary vs. Involuntary Social Withdrawal," *Journal of Gerontology*, 20 (1965) 363–71.

48. Irving Rosow, "Adjustment of the Normal Aged . . . ," in Richard Williams, Clark Tibbitts and Wilma Donahue (eds.), *Processes of Aging*, vol. 2 (New York: Atherton Press, 1963) 195–223.

mote a sense of identity. Indeed, the literature shows their sharp aversion to such memberships, especially when these are categorical.[49] This is in striking contrast to adolescents who generally find their peer groups compellingly attractive.[50] The acceptance of old age does not even offer the prospect of social redemption or some other gratifying alternative, such as appears among divorcees who commonly hope, through remarriage, to recover lost happiness, security, and social status. The very rejection of old age limits the possible support and other advantages that the elderly might get from peer groups.

Their antipathy is also intensified when age itself becomes a public issue, and they are evaluated and classified simply by ascription.[51] As is the case throughout the life cycle in America, their personal friends and associates are usually age peers.[52] They also regard friendship as a private matter that should not become the basis of public stigma or invidious social judgments. In this sense, they exempt their personal ties from public scrutiny and from ascriptive significance. This dichotomy between private and public lives minimizes the conflict that they might feel if they continued to accept the implications of earlier life styles in which one's friendships also symbolized one's social status.

However, their general antipathy to aging is directly related to the steady loss of prestige with which it is invested. If it were positively valued, they would have some incentive for a public identification with other elderly. But because they

---

49. Milton Barron, "Minority Group Characteristics of the Aged. . . ," *Journal of Gerontology*, 8 (1953) 477–82; Raphael Ginzberg, "The Negative Attitude toward the Elderly," *Geriatrics*, 7 (1952) 297–302; Nathan Kogan, "Attitudes toward Old People in an Older Sample," *Journal of Abnormal and Social Psychology*, 62 (1961) 616–22.

50. Talcott Parsons, "Age and Sex in the Social Structure of the United States," *American Sociological Review*, 7 (1942) 604–16.

51. Irving Rosow, *Social Integration of the Aged*, pp. 278–85.

52. *Ibid.*, pp. 69–75.

do not, older peers are not a positive reference group, either normatively or as a significant source of role models.[53] Insofar as the old apparently have no special set of new age norms, peers have no general standards for the approval or reward of expected new behavior. Older people simply have no distinctive role set—whether this consists of peers or not—which imposes new expectations on them.

This is also aggravated by the general reduction in their social participation. According to disengagement theory, this is part of a normal contraction of their world: presumably they withdraw from the social environment and the environment also excludes them.[54] Such withdrawal or exclusion is a sign of older people's alienation from the larger society. The peer group cannot effectively keep its members integrated in major role activity. While it may conceivably provide other bases of integration, it cannot offer access to central social roles.

Other differences in a trainee's relation to his peer group distinguish earlier from later status transitions. In earlier ones, the successful completion of training is usually marked by a public separation from the group, often ritually as in graduation ceremonies. This applies to all but a minority of failures, dropouts, or transfers who are separated quietly and nonritually. Typically, public separation signifies success and status gain, while private separation indicates failure or withdrawal. In old age, separation from a peer group usually occurs quietly and almost invariably indicates rejection or a loss of status. Withdrawal is an effort to reduce the various strains of participation, including those of illness, widowhood, re-

---

53. Harold Kelley, "Two Functions of Reference Groups," in Guy Swanson, Theodore Newcomb and Eugene Hartley (eds.), *Readings in Social Psychology*, rev. ed. (New York: Holt, 1952) 410–14.

54. Elaine Cumming and William Henry, *Growing Old* (New York: Basic Books, 1961); Elaine Cumming, Lois Dean and Isabel McCaffrey, "Disengagement—A Tentative Theory of Aging," *Sociometry*, 23 (1960) 25–35.

tirement, or serious loss of income. These are less important before old age because they are seldom so problematic. But as they become more frequent late in life, they also become the focus of social judgment. The failure of older people to meet the preferred criteria of minimal status loss is definitely associated with their withdrawal or exclusion from peer groups.[55] Further, the deviants or failures—who after all are only pioneers on a path all of their friends must eventually travel—are commonly viewed in stereotypical terms rather than in those individualized terms they were accustomed to earlier in life.[56] This ascriptive form of devaluation also serves to depersonalize the "failures." It indicates one major similarity of old and young groups: their limited tolerance of deviance from preferred standards.

Perhaps the most important structural difference between young and old peer groups in socialization is the complete breakdown of subgoals and goal gradients among the aged. This is strictly a function of aging as a process of social *loss*, so that socialization cannot be organized around social *growth* and acquisition. Hence, there are no significant subgoals that order role activity, nor are there goal gradients that stratify the peer group along lines of growing competence, whether by excellence or advancement. This distinction is present and vital in earlier socialization, but is completely absent in older groups. For with the dearth of new norms, the elderly cannot draw on their peers for subgoals or potential role models. Their major values cluster around the maintenance of youthfulness, the retention of roles, and the minimi-

---

55. Zena Blau, "Structural Constraints on Friendships in Old Age."
56. Milton Barron, "Minority Group Characteristics of the Aged . . ."; Nathan Kogan, *op. cit.*; Irving Rosow, "The Social Context of the Aging Self"; Jacob Tuckman, Irving Lorge and G. A. Spooner, "The Effect of Family Environment on Attitudes toward Old People and the Older Worker," *Journal of Social Psychology*, 38 (1953) 207–18; Irving Zola, "Feelings About Age Among Older People," *Journal of Gerontology*, 17 (1962) 65–68.

zation of change. With the erosion of time, their competence in these spheres cannot grow, no matter how the goals are graded.

YOUTHFUL NORMS

Here lies the crux of the entire socialization issue. It is not that older people actually lack any role models, real or potential, for they do have them. But these are not appropriate because they are primarily youthful models eminently disfunctional for the socialization to old age. The elderly judge themselves according to standards of youthfulness. This implies norms of minimal change, or preserving roles, activity, health, energy, beauty, vitality, and elan. The best life is presumably that which changes least from middle age.[57] This minimal change increases their chances of retaining social position, participation, prestige, and other advantages of middle age.

It has been argued that such youthful ideals are probably endemic in an advanced democratic society. Slater delineates three basic realities about aging in the modern world:[58]

> We cannot expect the prestige of the aged to be high in a society in which, as a group, they perform few important functions. . . . The functionlessness of the aged is a permanent fact of our society. . . . A high value on youth, or overestimation of youth, is inherent in a democratic society such as ours.

When the aged share these youthful ideals and models, there is no leverage for the major socialization pressure of *limiting rewards for adherence to previous standards and in-increasing rewards for conformity to new expectations.* For

---

57. Irving Rosow, "Adjustment of the Normal Aged . . ."
58. Philip Slater, "Cultural Attitudes toward the Aged," *Geriatrics*, 18 (1963) 308–14.

while the earlier norms are valued, the possible new ones are not. Therefore, rewards are not viable, they are not manipulated, and they have no effective function in the onset of old age. Admired models who may be emulated are precisely those who most successfully resist a change of their earlier life style and those who suffer the fewest physical or social stigmata of old age. Because there are widespread individual variations in these characteristics,[59] the most youthful, well-preserved aged are admired and emulated as exemplars of an indefinitely protracted middle age. In earlier socialization, the rewards lie in change; in old age, non-change is at a premium.

This should implicitly pose problems *within* the older population, but *apparently* mainly for the most deviant,[60] the "obsolete" whose physical, personal, and social characteristics are the least youthful. They feel the strain more heavily than the others. The basic problem of socialization to old age in America is the preparation for inevitable social losses and decline—the socialization to failure or obsolescence—with corresponding norms for a dignified life within those limitations. But America simply does not socialize effectively for any failure and seldom undertakes even to try.

However, this situation is somewhat misleading. Older people's youthful self-conceptions contrast sharply with younger persons' treatment of them. The elderly regard themselves as middle-aged while others see them as old. Flattering self-images may be psychologically sustaining for aging individuals if they are not challenged; but the cost of the discrepancy between private and public views of them may outweigh the advantages. Such discrepancies are inevitable sources of strain. They dramatize the generational differences

---

59. Leonard Breen, "The Aging Individual," in Clark Tibbitts (ed.), *Handbook of Social Gerontology* (Chicago: University of Chicago Press, 1960) 145–62.

60. Zena Blau, "Structural Constraints on Friendships in Old Age."

in perceptions of the elderly and the basis of younger people's indifference toward or deprecation of them.

Thereby, the discrepancy makes the problem of *social reality* paramount. If the elderly view themselves as middle-aged, but others see them as old, what is the social reality? What is their *social age*? Whose standards govern? Clearly, from the standpoint of sheer social power, younger generations are the standard-makers. If they consistently define people as old, they are socially old regardless of their health or similar factors. In accordance with the dictum of W. I. Thomas and Robert Merton, it becomes a self-fulfilling prophecy. Though their faculties and appearance may be well-preserved, when people are perceived and treated as elderly, this sets their social position. Therefore, the more persistently they try to maintain a youthful identity, the harder they rub against the abrasive negation of social reality. Such a gap between wish and reality inevitably imposes strains where there is little prospect for achieving the wish. The elderly can only maintain their private definitions at significant psychic cost, and there is small chance of reducing the source of strain. Nor can they halt their growing marginality and alienation from a society in which they strongly desire to remain integrated. Their youthful norms and role models conflict with the dominant conceptions of the culture. It is almost as if Ponce de Leon stepped through Alice in Wonderland's looking glass in pursuit of an ever receding fountain of youth and constantly reassured himself that he had found it—unto the grave. This is the crux of the dilemma of old age: the elderly want to remain relatively young, but the society will not let them. In this impasse, older people refuse to acknowledge and accept their social age. With no incentives or compelling pressures from the culture to embrace their age and no meaningful norms by which to live, they simply are not socialized to an aged role.

8. *The Prospect of Social Change*

To SUM UP the thrust of our analysis: The evidence of norms for old age is extremely weak and thin. Also, the situation of older people does not conform to the patterns that characterize socialization in other contexts. They are not embedded in a field that has the structure, processes, or effective variables typical of other settings. Accordingly, we may conclude that the evidence of tenuous norms for the aged is probably valid and that they are subject to only minor, flaccid socialization forces. Under these conditions, the chances of their socialization to an elderly role are negligible.

At this point, one may appropriately ask whether prospective social change might result in more refined norms and developed roles for the aged and thereby a more definite process of socialization. The question can be framed in three different terms: (1) the *changing attributes* of the elderly; (2) their *political activity*; and (3) the principles of *status allocation*. We will consider them briefly.

CHANGING ATTRIBUTES

Historical and institutional changes in twentieth century America have made each generation different from the cohorts that preceded it. Aside from subtler shifts in values and the conceptions of the good life, major changes among the contemporary aged are extremely clear in objective terms. There is a steady decline in ethnicity as the immigrant generation is dying away, so that by 1990 scarcely a handful of foreign language newspapers will be struggling to survive. But beyond this decline, there are also very genuine gains. Successive generations show significant improvements in longevity, health, education, and income. More people are reaching retirement in reasonably good vigor and health, with an expanding program of health services, such as Medicare, to keep them in good repair. The level of education and the interests correlated with this have steadily increased. Rising social security benefits and the proliferation of private pension plans give the aged both a greater income and the wherewithal to live. Therefore, successive generations of old people are better off than those that preceded them. Their material and objective situation has steadily improved.

But, paradoxically, the absolute gains of the aged may boil down to a situation of *relative* deprivation. For their various social benefits have increased at a rate *slower* than that of the nation as a whole. For example, educational standards and income are substantially higher for younger generations, with social security benefits growing at only one-third the rate of the net income of younger persons.[1] Thus, while the aged are better off in relation to their predecessors, they remain substantially disadvantaged in comparison with their younger *contemporaries*. Their absolute improvements

---

1. For a discussion of the relative income status of older people, see Irving Rosow, *Social Integration of the Aged* (New York: Free Press, 1967) 14–20.

simply mean that, in sharing the benefits of economic growth, they are falling behind at a slower pace than earlier generations. Accordingly, in terms of a pro rata share of expanding social values, the old remain disadvantaged, and their future prospects offer little promise of significant improvement.

Under these conditions, there seems to be little effective leverage for new roles or norms to emerge for the old. For there is little viable basis for this in new responsibilities, significant social functions, or ideological commitment. And the changing attributes of the aged promise to have little effect on this situation.

POLITICAL ACTIVITY

A persistent suggestion has raised the prospect of the elderly exacting a greater share of social values through militant political action. In terms of organized political behavior, this poses some serious difficulties. It would require them to adopt an embarrassing, invidious public stance, and it also presupposes a sharp discontinuity in the principles of political affiliation.[2] While these conditions are by no means impossible to meet, it seems quite unlikely for the aged, who are so much more heterogeneous than other militant minorities.

But even if they were able to organize politically and successfully advance their interests, this in itself would not necessarily assure the genesis of new roles and norms beyond those of the political mobilization itself. In other words, political pressure might exact somewhat greater intrinsic shares in the pool of social values without significantly affecting the other terms of their social participation and integration. Minor material concessions do not necessarily imply major social redefinitions, so the normative ambiguities might well remain relatively undisturbed.

---

2. Irving Rosow, "Old Age: One Moral Dilemma of an Affluent Society," *Gerontologist*, 2 (1962) 182–91.

STATUS ALLOCATION

The final aspect of potential social change involves our mode of evaluating people and allocating status. The possibility is mooted that our growing awareness of and concern with the aged (and other disadvantaged groups) signifies a change of national heart in which we acknowledge more of their moral claims in our distribution of values. While this might not accord them significantly greater honor, presumably it should mitigate the stigma of aging and the invidiousness of their social position.[3]

This argument or hope poses two difficulties. First, it does not address the main issue of role development and normative specification that would be relevant to prospective socialization. As with political activity, it does not necessarily follow that increasing old people's benefits and easing the antipathy to aging would result in more articulated roles and norms—much less in greater responsibility and a substantially tighter integration into the society. The possible loosening of invidious judgments does not imply major gains in prestige, much less the development of significant roles and expectations that would be grist for the socialization mill.

Second, the argument ignores the fundamental principles underlying our stratification system and its allocation of status. We value and reward people mainly in accordance with their *economic utility*. A person's social class position and relative prestige are ultimately anchored in the occupational structure, which makes social standing largely dependent on work roles. Indeed, even scarce skills and qualities

---

3. In one study of the relative odium of twenty-one physical disabilities, old age stood exactly at the midpoint in ranking, nestled neatly between cancer and paraplegia. It is regarded more benignly than alcoholism and mental illness, but less so than blindness or stroke. More significant certainly is the sheer fact that aging can simply be construed without comment to be a disability. Cf. John Tringo, "The Hierarchy of Preference Toward Disability Groups," *Journal of Special Education*, 4 (1970) 295–306.

such as athletic ability or unusual beauty are most negotiable
and rewarded after they have been converted to marketable
form. Thus, the flow of prestige and status is primarily governed by economic values and functions. From this standpoint, the aged are severely disadvantaged, especially after
retirement, and economic and technological changes are pe-
nalizing them further. For the pace of change accelerates the
rate at which increasing segments of successive generations
become economically obsolete and unessential.[4]

For the elderly to realize significant *status* benefits from
a more benign human vision would require a profound transformation of our basic institutions. Because the aged have
declining economic and social functions, they would have to
be valued on grounds other than performance. This would
call for a drastic decline in the Protestant ethic and its emphasis on competition, productivity, achievement, and economic utility. Thereby prestige and honor might be distrib-
uted according to new principles of virtue and worth. In a
status system based on intrinsic human qualities, people could
be evaluated and rewarded for their attributes and relationships rather than for their performances. Much of the current
political agitation of youth and the social protest of the coun-
ter-culture is ostensibly based on such a perspective. This
pressure may well be loosening up our institutions a bit, with
some modification and reknitting of norms around the edges.
But it has its limitations, for many of the changes have been
more cosmetic than fundamental. There is little evidence
that massive social forces are gathering for a revolutionary
transformation of the stratification system or the principles
governing the allocation of social status. There is little reason

4. For a detailed analysis of the larger problem of old age and
status allocation, see Irving Rosow, "Retirement Leisure and Social
Status," in Duke University Council on Aging and Human Development,
Proceedings of Seminars, 1965–1969 (Durham, N.C.: Duke University
Center for the Study of Aging and Human Development, 1969) 249–57.

to expect the early decline of economic utility as the major determinate of prestige or to believe that the position of older people will be drastically altered on the basis of such a change.

Of course, one might postulate a revision of those basic American values that now exclude the aged and submit them to indifference or denigration. But this would be unrealistic and artificial, a *deus ex machina*. It would deny the fundamental character of our institutions that certainly can be expected to continue for at least the short-term future and probably longer.

In summary, there is little immediate promise of social change that would integrate the elderly more tightly into our society. There is no prospect of a significant increase in their social responsibilities and functions or of the development of clearer norms and roles for them. Accordingly, there is little likelihood of a strong process of socialization to old age, either in our present institutional context or in a new kind of framework that might reasonably be expected to emerge.

9. *Alternatives: A Theoretical Derivation*

LET US make two assumptions: (1) that our basic institutions continue to devalue and exclude the elderly, and (2) that socialization to an aged role is desirable. With these clear premises, we may now pose the problem of socialization in terms of possible alternatives within the *present* institutional structure. If the conventional forces of socialization are weak, are there special conditions in our society, perhaps atypical and scattered in various niches and interstices in the system, which are conducive to the development of norms and roles to which older people might be socialized, even in localized or parochial terms? This is the issue that the rest of this analysis will address.

One set of conditions might present a viable socialization alternative. This might not only reduce the strains of discrepant public and private images of older persons, but also weaken the obstacles and facilitate socialization to new aged roles. The critical factor, as a necessary if not sufficient condition, is the *insulation* of the elderly from other age groups and their increased association with age peers. This represents two essential conditions: (1) the reduction of contact and weakening of ties with younger people, and (2) the concentration of socially similar older persons within a local setting, preferably residential. There is ample evidence that such arrangements would create strong friendship groups that would protect the aged from the negative definitions of the larger society.[1] In other words, if their lives were largely organized within homogeneous peer groups, this might reduce the effects of conflicting reference groups and ease the strains of their discrepant self-images and crumbling status.[2] And other results might also be expected.

What does this really involve? Essentially it implies a shift in older people's orientation and participation from *exclusive* to *inclusive* social settings. Several predictable effects of this change would also reinforce each other. Shifting their involvements from arenas of negative to those of positive attitudes would insulate the elderly from denigration. Further, loosening their bonds from rejecting groups and transferring them to accepting groups would reduce the discrepancy between their self-images and others' invidious perceptions of them. In addition, simply belonging to a homogeneous social group would in itself be salutary, for aside from any other factor, members of homogeneous groups tend to have higher self-esteem than those of heterogeneous groups.[3] These conditions would facilitate normal group supports, one of which

---

1. Irving Rosow, *Social Integration of the Aged*, (New York: Free Press, 1967).

2. This should not be misconstrued as a social policy recommendation for the arbitrary separation of generations in the population, although considerable segregation of young families occurs as a result of the real estate market. Our present concern is to specify those conditions conducive to the social reintegration of older people who are subject to alienation from their society.

3. Morris Rosenberg, "The Dissonant Religious Context and Emotional Disturbance," *American Journal of Sociology*, 68 (1962) 1–10.

warrants special mention. The fairly irreversible attrition of social roles (marital, work, etc.) has isolating effects that might be partially compensated through friendships and informal associations. Here Arnold Rose's analysis of aging subcultures and group consciousness, which we considered earlier, becomes particularly relevant.[4] Or, as another analyst of deviance stated:[5]

> Even in the absence of an already established deviant culture and social organization, a number of individuals with like problems and *in effective communication with one another* may join together to do what no one can do alone. They may provide one another with reference objects, collectively contrive a subculture to replace or neutralize the conventional culture, and support and shield one another in their deviance.

Exactly! Note, however, that this is predicated on both effective communication and a viable group life. These are the minimum conditions for the development of new group norms and expectations from which new roles might well be fashioned. It is more important that these norms are simply *shared* by the group, even if they be *peculiar* to it, and less important that they may differ from those of the larger society. Under these circumstances, an alternative to rolelessness is clearly feasible, even though its scope might be extremely narrow and localized.

There is, of course, no assurance that a high concentration of the aged would necessarily have such significant effects on their lives, though the available evidence is persuasive. Their incentive to identify with old peers might still remain weak, so that local concentrations of socially similar elderly might not always generate cohesive groups or effective

---

4. Cf. *supra*.
5. Albert Cohen, "The Sociology of the Deviant Act: Anomie Theory and Beyond," *American Sociological Review*, 30 (1965) 5–14 (italics inserted).

socializing systems. That might be a necessary, but not sufficient condition for socialization to an aged role. This poses
both theoretical and empirical issues: to specify the factors that favor their identification and socialization, and to
describe the kinds of people who do and do not become
socialized.

To illustrate, let us consider one significant group of
possible role models: the relatively younger aged whose decrements from middle age are still minor, but who have nonetheless been *socially redefined as old*. Their personal youthfulness makes them the most qualified leaders and potential
role models for their older peers *if youthful norms should
persist* for the elderly. They would probably be the significant
reference figures for the others. But from the standpoint of
these youthful old leaders, who would *their* reference figures
be—their old peers or younger persons? It is quite problematic whom they would choose. Would they prefer the esteem
and response of their aged compatriots? Or would they steadfastly dissociate themselves from the elderly in favor of a marginal participation in the larger society? Would they opt for
a peripheral, neglected place near the mainstream or an influ-
ential position in a devalued group? Which reference group
would the youthful potential leaders pick, their age mates or
younger persons?[6]

If they should opt for younger persons and eschew their
peers, obviously they would have few functions in modeling
or socialization. But if they should decide to associate with
the elderly, this would not assure socialization to a distinctive
aged role if the group continued to function with *youthful*
norms. At best, the group could only *insulate* its members

---

6. Insofar as the alternatives also involve a choice of status system
in which they place themselves, there are elements here of Merton's distinction between locals and cosmopolitans. Cf. Robert Merton, *Social
Theory and Social Structure*, rev. ed. (Glencoe: Free Press, 1957) 387–
420.

somewhat from the effects of the larger society. It could only provide a buffer against the general repudiation of old people's mutual flattery, the challenge to the terms of their reciprocity, the dissent from the youthfulness, vigor, competence, wisdom, and grace with which they so generously endow and support each other. Thus, a cohesive group might reduce the abrasion of social reality through a quiet form of collusive denial. If external contradictions were limited, then the members' privately shared norms might operate freely within the group. Thereby, despite their rejection outside, members could support each other and their own belief system.

This presupposes that such groups would function as many elites do, maintaining their boundaries by strongly exclusive associations. Limited access and concentrated interaction would serve to insulate such groups from the environment, both objectively and in the minds of their members. Under these conditions, they can sustain private norms and images of themselves which differ from those of the larger social order, somewhat in the fashion of pariah peoples who regard themselves as chosen or low caste groups that disavow their invidious ranking.

This clearly indicates *how* deviant standards can be maintained. Obviously, this structure might stabilize youthful norms by creating a sheltered private world that can preserve older people's desires and illusions. In this vein, Zena Blau observes, "This stability of the network of relationships within a group of [aged] friends or co-workers prevents mutual awareness of gradual alterations that take place in each of the participants," especially after age seventy.[7] Thus, the peer group is an excellent mechanism for the collusive denial of age and the persistence of quasi-youthful norms. It may not silence, but it certainly muffles disruptive questions or re-

7. Zena Blau, "Changes in Status and Age Identification," *American Sociological Review*, 21 (1956) 198–203.

joinders from the outside. Within the group, it may convert a social fiction from a charade to a limited social reality in the fashion of *Enrico IV* and other plays of Pirandello. This is precisely the model of social organization that appears in various retirement villages or other geriatric centers such as Miami.

However, while they might persist under such conditions, *youthful norms do not create new aged roles*, nor do they foster identification with them. Indeed, enclaves of the elderly can support deviance and militate against a new socialization. Yet socialization to old age fundamentally requires something different: the formulation of a distinctive new role,[8] new expectations and norms appropriate to it, and a set of eligible role models. So the problem is whether and how youthful standards could change in our society. Under what conditions could norms develop which would be conducive to socialization?

Given our basic premises, the required changes could only originate within older peer groups. But for these to become positive reference groups in *non-youthful* terms, they would also have to be viable social groups that serve other major functions for their members.

Such groups should coalesce and thrive under two basic conditions. First, when the members are also *socially homogeneous on factors other than age*, notably social class, race, ethnicity, and marital status. In other words, the factors that normally govern voluntary social groupings and spontaneous association. Thereby, the force of group attractiveness would depend not simply on one shared characteristic of the members—age—but on many other similarities as well: social position, life situation, experience, problems, interests, tastes, life styles, and so on. The integrating power of these similarities is proportional to the number that members share. Even

---

8. Warren Roland, "Cultural, Personal and Situational Roles," *Sociology and Social Research*, 34 (September–October, 1949) 104–11.

special interest groups are most viable when they are based on normal principles of voluntary association and most cohesive when members are bound to the group by many ties rather than a few. Accordingly, these other basic similarities should continue to be strong and reinforce the incipient solidarity of age peers.[9] Thereby, age would be only one of several or many social bonds, not the primary basis of the group's identity and function.

The second condition favorable to such groups is *large concentrations* of similar elderly. This is purely an ecological factor that takes into account the steady contraction of old people's life space[10] and their growing dependence on the immediate local environment for stable social contact.[11] Such dependence on local resources generally increases with age,[12] particularly with declining health, so that sheer proximity, accessibility, and convenience become significant limiting conditions of their social participation.

Social structures that meet these two conditions cannot guarantee the formation of cohesive groups of the elderly, but by setting favorable circumstances, they would virtually assure it. Nor would they assimilate all the local aged. For some

9. Although there is evidence that migration may vitiate the force of these factors in the social life of retirement centers, this may well be a function of both the conditions of migrant life and the self-selection of older migrants rather than the general change in determinates of association. Cf. Ernest Burgess, "Social Relations, Activities and Personal Adjustment," *American Journal of Sociology*, 59 (1954) 352–60; G. C. Hoyt, "The Life of the Retired in a Trailer Park," *American Journal of Sociology*, 59 (1954) 361–70; L. C. Michelon, "The New Leisure Class," *American Journal of Sociology*, 59 (1954) 371–78.

10. Elaine Cumming and William Henry, *Growing Old* (New York: Basic Books, 1961); Elaine Cumming, Lois Dean and Isabel McCaffrey, "Disengagement—A Tentative Theory of Aging," *Sociometry*, 23 (1960) 25–35.

11. Wendell Bell and Marion Boat, "Urban Neighborhoods and Informal Social Relations," *American Journal of Sociology*, 62 (1957) 391–98; Joel Smith, William Form and Gregory Stone, "Local Intimacy in a Middle-Sized City," *American Journal of Sociology*, 60 (1954) 276–84.

12. Irving Rosow, *Social Integration of the Aged*.

are externally oriented and avoid local involvements;[13] others, because of excessive passivity, cannot be effectively integrated in a group despite their desire for friendships.[14] The critical element, however, is that the concentration of similar old people maximizes *social opportunities*, the chances for interaction, and the prospect of flourishing local groups.

Such friendships would not necessarily isolate the aged from their previous networks, as in some formal socialization situations. But they might eventually come to approximate this if they were successful in protecting their members from the invidious judgments of others and in providing them with important satisfactions that they received nowhere else.

PEER GROUP FUNCTIONS

If such groups were not bound by youthful norms, they should develop some major socializing mechanisms.[15] Many of these inhere in the basic functions that groups commonly perform for their members. Some are quite conventional. But others are strategic for the socialization to old age because

---

13. *Ibid.*, pp. 108–10.
14. *Ibid.*, pp. 112–13, 118–22.
15. Ernest Burgess (ed.), *Retirement Villages* (Ann Arbor: University of Michigan, Division of Gerontology, 1961), and Ernest Burgess, "Social Relations, Activities and Personal Adjustment"; G. C. Hoyt, *op. cit.*; Robert Kleemeier, "An Analysis of Patterns of Group Living for Older People," in Irving Webber (ed.), *Aging: A Current Appraisal* (Gainesville: University of Florida Press, 1956), 167–79, and "Environmental Settings and the Aging Process," in John Anderson (ed.), *Psychological Aspects of Aging* (Washington: American Psychological Association, 1956), 105–16, and "Moosehaven: Congregate Living in a Community of the Retired," *American Journal of Sociology*, 59 (1954) 347–51; L. C. Michelon, *op. cit.*; Arnold Rose, "Group Consciousness among the Aging," in Arnold Rose and Warren Peterson (eds.), *Older People and their Social World* (Philadelphia: F. A. Davis, 1965) 19–36; Irving Rosow, "Retirement Housing and Social Integration," *Gerontologist*, 1 (1961) 85–91, also in Clark Tibbitts and Wilma Donahue (eds.), *Social and Psychological Aspects of Aging* (New York: Columbia University Press, 1962) 327–40; Irving Webber, *op. cit.*

other institutions simply do not provide them for the elderly. Accordingly, we will briefly review those peer group functions that are particularly significant for their socialization.

Group Support

Foremost of these functions is sheer *group support*. The more attractive the group and the deeper one's embeddedness in it, the greater the support that it can provide its members. One aspect of group support is help in time of illness or trouble. This is especially important for the more vulnerable older persons whose resources for meeting various crises may be dwindling.

New Group Memberships

Second, one particular support may concentrate specifically on the crisis of role change itself. When the actor is cut off from former roles, his transition to a new status is facilitated by *new group memberships*. They not only cushion the transition itself and make it complete, they also replace old memberships that are lost. Significantly, this support would most commonly be provided by people who have experienced or are currently undergoing the same crisis. They are personally familiar with the stresses, problems, and anxieties that beset the new member. Those who have previously gone through the transition are experienced enough to help interpret the strains and set them in perspective and to advise on how to cope with them. When such adjustment problems take interim form and develop as "phases" in a transition process, they may be the functional equivalents of goal gradients in which those who are more experienced and advanced can help the novices. Hence, the group has adaptive value insofar as the more advanced peers help to indoctrinate newcomers.

New Role Set

Third, when the individual joins a new group, its members become the core of a *new role set*. To the extent that they share his position and a common relation to others, their perspective can facilitate his role transition. While a person sometimes regards his problems as if they were unique (and old people often suffer their strains in isolation), he can and does see when they are actually shared by others. This common perspective adumbrates any former status differences among members and emphasizes the similarities in their current situation. These shared attributes and the social homogeneity they signify are intrinsically integrative forces. As a nascent role set, such an aged group offers the prospect of new friends and associates to replace those that have been lost or will soon wither away. This contains elements of both role set replacement and abridgement.[16] Consistent with this, even new elderly neighbors become a stronger reference group to the aged than their old friends who are not neighbors.[17]

Role Specification

Fourth, all groups develop norms that deal with the relationships and problems common to their members. Accordingly, membership in a group of the elderly generates considerable pressure for *role specification*. Especially with the present openness and ambiguity of an aged role, peer groups can crystallize norms and expectations that begin to structure a more definite, clear role.[18] If aging itself is a major

---

16. Robert Merton, *Social Theory and Social Structure*, 379.
17. Irving Rosow, *Social Integration of the Aged*, 176–84.
18. Leonard Cottrell, "Adjustment of the Individual to his Age and Sex Roles," *American Sociological Review*, 7 (1942) 617–20; Arnold Rose, *Theory and Method in the Social Sciences* (Minneapolis: University of Minnesota Press, 1954).

bond and basis of group cohesion, and if normative expectations are the major cultural vacuum, then the role of an elderly person is implicitly a prime focus of group concern. The efforts become significant to clarify and solve members' adaptive problems, to pattern their activities and relationships. For the group is involved in the refinement of standards and judgments about a range of concerns which ultimately refer to members in role terms. Norms are generated which are usually role-centered and certainly role-relevant. The substance of these adaptive patterns and their implicit values are in essence role specifications.

In the absence of general cultural expectations about old age, such emerging norms are clearly subject to great variation among local older groups. This is inevitable. Indeed, some of them might even cleave to youthful standards; but most probably would not. However, in terms of the normative variation, there is certainly ample room for different definitions among groups. If the consensus about role specification were to be compared with that found at earlier life stages, the variation might be greater for some central roles (e.g., spouse), but no more than for others (e.g., sundry work or leisure groups). But the lack of consensus among groups is not particularly problematic so long as standards are reasonably clear within them. For local norms provide the basis of socialization, even though the roles themselves might vary from one group to another.

Positive Reference Group

Fifth, the net result of the foregoing group functions is to make peers a *positive reference group*. Through them, older people can identify with their age mates much more than they do at present. As with other reference groups, this one would also mediate members' adjustment to the norms.

Insulation of Members

Sixth, those groups should be highly salient to their members. They offer some solid gratifications; and with relatively weak involvements elsewhere (aside from their family), older people should be strongly attached to these groups. Accordingly, when they are firmly anchored and embedded, the group can provide considerable *insulation of its members* from invidious judgments and conflicting standards from outside. While it cannot shield them completely from exposure, indifference, or devaluation, it can reduce these and minimize their effects, just as other deviant or pariah groups shelter their members from the antipathy of the larger society. As we have observed, such insulation from external pressures or competing reference figures limits conflicts and promotes socialization.

Qualified Role Models

Seventh, under these conditions, the group also provides its members with a set of *qualified role models*. These may be leaders who best personify major group values; they may be others who have most successfully met the special configuration of problems that a given person faces; or they may be an ideal composite of characteristics of several admired members. Because these models are immediately available in the group, we can call them proximate. They have some major advantages over other possible models in socialization:[19] (a) They are *real* rather than imaginary figures. (b) They are *personal* friends or associates rather than strangers or remote figures. (c) They are *average* rather than exceptional older people, such as Albert Schweitzer, Eleanor Roosevelt, or Bertrand Russell whom well-meaning advisors often encourage the ordinary aged to emulate. (d) They are quite likely

---

19. Cf. Irving Rosow, *Social Integration of the Aged*, 139–46.

to be fairly *complete* rather than partial or truncated models for an older person. Consequently, proximate models are real and close, and direct contact with them promotes socialization.[20] The model's attributes are clear and realistic and can be checked. The gap between the actor and model in space, time, or capacity is minimal, and this stimulates identification that is not fanciful, but meaningful and consequential in the context of the actor's life. Accordingly, the model is immediately relevant to the solution of current problems, some of them pressing, and does not implicitly symbolize some vague future state.

New Self-Images

Finally, the circumstances that favor identification also promote *new self-images*. These are not only intrinsic to socialization; in the present case, they probably make possible and ease the genuine acceptance of one's age. This is contingent, of course, on the group's definition of fairly clear norms and appropriate roles for the elderly.

In the socialization alternative we have postulated, the crucial conditions are the anchorage of old people in a group of similar peers and their insulation from conflicting external norms and definitions. Unless these provisions are met, it is doubtful that the group can develop deviant standards that are viable and can long survive the weight of prevailing cultural views. Such a peer group can only overcome the stigma of aging when it becomes structurally self-contained, strongly bounded, vital to its members, and significantly resistant to external pressures. Membership and group support not only promise the older person a clearer social identity, but also become significant rewards that strengthen his dependence

---

20. Leonard Cottrell, "Adjustment of the Individual to his Age and Sex Roles"; and "Some Neglected Problems in Social Psychology," *American Sociological Review*, 15 (1950) 709–11.

on the group and his ties to it. They would also introduce to aging the first functional equivalent of the gains in status found in transitions earlier in life. Thus, our alternative establishes the necessary conditions for effective socialization to an aged role; whether this would be sufficient awaits further study.

This presupposes that the present alienation of old people from society will continue fundamentally unchanged. Our current institutions and values do not offer a choice between marginality and integration of the aged, but simply between alternative forms of alienation. Even though older people now accept prevailing beliefs and values, they are still alienated from significant social participation, they enjoy no respected place, and they have little group support beyond the immediate family. There are at present no effective norms, leverage nor incentives for their socialization to an aged role. But in the alternative proposed here, their larger alienation would be buffered by a supportive group, a deviant enclave of social integration. Under these conditions, we would expect a significant development of aged roles and effective socialization to them—even though the norms might be consensual within groups, but variable between them, and deviant in the larger society.

SOME RECENT EVIDENCE

Since this analysis was completed, it has received impressive support in a recently published independent study. Arlie Hochschild conducted a three-year participant observation project in the San Francisco area of the residents of Merrill Court, a small public housing project of senior citizens, mainly widows of working-class background.[21] This enclave met our fundamental condition of a *concentration of*

---

21. Arlie Hochschild, *The Unexpected Community* (Englewood Cliffs, N.J.: Prentice-Hall, 1973).

socially homogeneous members, not only on age, but also on sex, marital status, social class, regional background, and in many cases on religion and elements of personal history. Her description and rich qualitative data provide a welcome supplement to the numerous surveys available in the literature.

Basically, Hochschild observed and documented in rich detail a thriving, bubbling cauldron of local community life with all the features predicted independently by our analysis. She entered an established community and could not describe the *process* by which new local norms developed. Nor did she focus her research specifically on socialization.[22] But she did find that a strong body of normative expectations had developed, and there were clear standards by which residents judged appropriate participation in the public and private life of Merrill Court. The eight group functions that we identified as distinctively significant for socialization all appeared. There were new group memberships, a new role set, clear role prescriptions, positive new reference groups, abundant role models, solid self-images, extremely strong group support and reciprocity, and the insulation of members not only from invidious external judgments, but also the weakening of kinship and other external ties. In other words, the residents developed a strong consensus around central values that became the basis for role expectations in a sharply bounded group. And their norms were supported by the classic social pressures typical of highly cohesive small groups or villages. Not only were role standards articulated and supported through

---

22. One formal study has been undertaken on socialization in a retirement center. But its value is limited by a basic misunderstanding of the concept of socialization, falling into the common hazard of confusing socialization with "good adjustment." It also treats lack of change as more important than change in the acquisition of new roles: "Activity which helped him *sustain* his [former] identity could be viewed as contributing to his socialization to old age, regardless [of] . . . whether new social learning was required." Cf. Mary Seguin, "Opportunity for Peer Socialization in a Retirement Community," *Gerontologist*, 13 (1973) 208–14.

rewards and social controls, but other features of cohesive groups also developed: rituals, taboos, private humor, mutual aid, and so on. The values, group embeddedness, and roles enabled the members to meet certain problems of aging more successfully than other old people, like themselves, who lived outside:

> The residents of Merrill Court are not a collection of individuals, but a community. Collectively they have devised a solution to one of the most crucial problems of old age—loneliness (6f.). . . . The widows, insulated by a community of older peers, feel the sting of stigma less than most isolated older people (136).

While Hochschild was not immediately concerned with issues of socialization as such, her account makes plain that when the conditions we have specified are met, norms are generated, roles developed, and a process of socialization does occur. Her data are most encouraging for the alternative we have proposed and indicate that the fundamental line of analysis is probably correct. Its details remain to be refined in future research.

The socialization to old age is important as a specific problem in a more general theory of adult socialization. The socialization to any devalued status or group is theoretically significant, and the elderly represent the prospective socialization to social obsolescence, loss, and implicit failure. For older people do not now exemplify the successfully socialized members of various minority groups (e.g., ethnic or racial) or of deviant subcultures (e.g., homosexual, delinquent, criminal, or hippie). Rather, they are persons who for various reasons are not successfuly socialized to statuses, usually devalued, which they *do* occupy. Such instances cover many situations in which socialization, especially outside custodial institutions, has varying effectiveness. This presents the following theoretical problem: to clarify the difficulty of socializing to some devalued positions (e.g., the aged), but not to others (e.g., juvenile delinquents or hippies). The present analysis has taken only the first step in that direction; for this purpose, the aged represent a distinctive limiting case for theory.

Bibliography

Aberle, David, *et al.* "The Functional Prerequisites of a Society," *Ethics*, 9 (1950) 100–11.

Aldridge, Gordon. "Informal Social Relationships in a Retirement Community," *Marriage and Family Living*, 21 (1959) 70–72.

Anderson, Nancy. "The Significance of Age Categories for Older Persons," *Gerontologist*, 7 (1967) 164–67.

Arensberg, Conrad, and Solon Kimball. *Family and Community in Ireland* (Cambridge: Harvard University Press, 1940).

Axelrod, Morris. "Urban Structure and Social Participation," *American Sociological Review*, 21 (1956) 13–18.

Bailey, F. G. "Closed Social Stratification in India," *European Journal of Sociology*, 4 (1963) 107–24.

Bailyn, Lotte, and Herbert Kelman. "The Effects of a Year's Experience in America in the Self-Image of Scandinavians," *Journal of Social Issues*, 18, 1 (1962) 30–40.

Barron, Milton. "The Dynamics of Occupational Roles and Health in Old Age," in John Anderson (ed.), *Psychological Aspects of Aging* (Washington: American Psychological Association, 1956) 236–39.

———. "Minority Group Characteristics of the Aged in American Society," *Journal of Gerontology*, 8 (1953) 477–82.

Becker, Ernest. "Socialization, Command of Performance, and Mental Illness," *American Journal of Sociology*, 67 (1962) 494–501.

Becker, Howard. "Notes on the Concept of Commitment," *American Journal of Sociology*, 66 (1960) 32–40.

———. "Personal Change in Adult Life," *Sociometry*, 27 (1964) 40–53.

Becker, Howard, and James Carper. "The Development of Identification with an Occupation," *American Journal of Sociology*, 61 (1956) 289–98.

———. "The Elements of Identification with an Occupation," *American Sociological Review*, 21 (1956) 341–48.

Becker, Howard, and Blanche Geer. "The Fate of Idealism in Medical School," *American Sociological Review*, 23 (1958) 50–56.

Becker, Howard, Blanche Geer, Everett Hughes, and Anselm Strauss. *Boys in White* (Chicago: University of Chicago Press, 1961).

Bell, Wendell, and Marion Boat. "Urban Neighborhoods and Informal Social Relations," *American Journal of Sociology*, 62 (1957) 391–98.

Bell, Wendell, and Maryanne Force. "Urban Neighborhood Types and Participation in Formal Associations," *American Sociological Review*, 21 (1956) 25–34.

Bellin, Seymour, and Louis Kriesberg. "Relationship Among Attitudes, Circumstances, and Behavior: The Case of Applying for Public Housing," *Sociology and Social Research*, 51 (1967) 453–69.

Benedict, Ruth. "Continuities and Discontinuities in Cultural Conditioning," *Psychiatry*, 1 (1938) 161–67.

Berg, Philip. "Adult Socialization and Social Work Practice," *Social Work*, 12 (1967) 89–94.

Berreman, Gerald. "Caste in India and the United States," *American Journal of Sociology*, 66 (1960) 120–27.

Bettelheim, Bruno. "Individual and Mass Behavior in Extreme Situations," *Journal of Abnormal and Social Psychology*, 38 (1943) 417–52.

Biderman, Albert. "The Image of 'Brainwashing,' " *Public Opinion Quarterly*, 26 (1962) 547–63.

Blau, Peter. *Exchange and Power in Social Life* (New York: John Wiley, 1964).

———. "Occupational Bias and Mobility," *American Sociological Review*, 22 (1957) 392–99.

———. "Social Mobility and Interpersonal Relations," *American Sociological Review*, 21 (1956) 290–95.

Blau, Zena. "Changes in Status and Age Identification," *American Sociological Review*, 21 (1956) 198–203.

―――. "Structural Constraints on Friendships in Old Age," *American Sociological Review*, 26 (1961) 429–39.

Bredemeier, Harry, and Richard Stephenson. *The Analysis of Social Systems* (New York: Holt, Rinehart & Winston, 1962).

Breen, Leonard. "The Aging Individual," in Clark Tibbitts (ed.), *Handbook of Social Gerontology* (Chicago: University of Chicago Press, 1960) 145–62.

Brim, Orville. "Adult Socialization," in John Clausen (ed.), *Socialization and Society* (Boston: Little, Brown, 1968) 186–226.

Brim, Orville, and Stanton Wheeler. *Socialization After Childhood* (New York: John Wiley, 1966).

Burgess, Ernest. "Personal and Social Adjustment in Old Age," in Milton Derber (ed.), *The Aged and Society* (Champaign, Ill.: Industrial Relations Research Association, 1950) 138–56.

―――. (ed.). *Retirement Villages* (Ann Arbor: University of Michigan, Division of Gerontology, 1961).

―――. "Social Relations, Activities and Personal Adjustment," *American Journal of Sociology*, 59 (1954) 352–60.

Cavan, Ruth. "Family Life and Family Substitutes in Old Age," *American Sociological Review*, 14 (1949) 71–83.

Chandler, Albert. "The Traditional Chinese Attitude toward Old Age," *Journal of Gerontology*, 4 (1949) 239–44.

Chapanis, Natalie and Alphonse. "Cognitive Dissonance: Five Years Later," *Psychological Bulletin*, 61 (1964) 1–22.

Chellam, Grace. "Disengagement Theory: Awareness of Death and Self-Engagement" (Unpub. D.S.W. Thesis, Case Western Reserve University, 1964).

Clausen, John (ed.). *Socialization and Society* (Boston: Little, Brown, 1968).

Cogswell, Betty. "Rehabilitation of the Paraplegic: Processes of Socialization," *Sociological Inquiry*, 37 (Winter, 1967) 11–26.

Cohen, Albert. "The Sociology of the Deviant Act: Anomie Theory and Beyond," *American Sociological Review*, 30 (1965) 5–14.

Coker, Robert, *et al.* "Patterns of Influence: Medical School Faculty Members and the Values and Specialty Interests of Medical Students," *Journal of Medical Education*, 35 (1960) 518–27.

Coser, Rose. "Insulation from Observability and Types of Social Conformity," *American Sociological Review*, 25 (1961) 28–39.

———. "Role Distance, Sociological Ambivalence, and Transitional Status Systems," *American Journal of Sociology*, 72 (1966) 173–87.

Cottrell, Leonard. "Adjustment of the Individual to his Age and Sex Roles," *American Sociological Review*, 7 (1942) 617–20.

———. "Some Neglected Problems in Social Psychology," *American Sociological Review*, 15 (1950) 709–11.

Coutu, Walter. "Role-Playing vs. Role-Taking," *American Sociological Review*, 16 (1951) 180–87.

Cumming, Elaine, and William Henry. *Growing Old* (New York: Basic Books, 1961).

Cumming, Elaine, Lois Dean, and Isabel McCaffrey. "Disengagement—A Tentative Theory of Aging," *Sociometry*, 23 (1960) 25–35.

Davis, Fred. "Deviance Disavowal: The Management of Strained Interaction by the Visibly Handicapped," *Social Problems*, 9 (Winter, 1961) 120–32.

Davis, Kingsley. "The Sociology of Parent-Youth Conflict," *American Sociological Review*, 5 (1940) 523–35.

Davis, Robert. "The Relationship of Social Preferability to Self-Concept in an Aged Population," *Journal of Gerontology*, 17 (1962) 431–36.

Day, Robert, and Robert Hamblin. "Some Effects of Close and Punitive Styles of Supervision," *American Journal of Sociology*, 69 (1964) 499–510.

Deutsch, Morton, and Leonard Solomon. "Reactions to Evaluations by Others as Influenced by Self-Evaluations," *Sociometry*, 22 (1959) 93–112.

Donahue, Wilma, Woodrow Hunter, and Dorothy Coons. "Study of the Socialization of Old People," *Geriatrics*, 8 (1953) 656–66.

Donahue, Wilma, Harold Orbach, and Otto Pollak. "Retirement: The Emerging Social Pattern," in Clark Tibbitts (ed.), *Handbook of Social Gerontology* (Chicago: University of Chicago Press, 1960) 330–406.

Downing, Joseph. "Factors Affecting the Selective Use of a Social Club for the Aged," *Journal of Gerontology*, 12 (1957) 81–84.

Drake, Joseph. "Some Factors Influencing Students' Attitudes toward Older People," *Social Forces*, 35 (1957) 266–71.

Durkheim, Emile. *The Division of Labor in Society* (Glencoe: Free Press, 1947).

Eckhardt, Kenneth, and Gerry Hendershot. "Dissonance, Congruence and the Perception of Public Opinion," *American Journal of Sociology*, 73 (1967) 222–34.

Ellis, Robert, and W. Clayton Lane. "Social Mobility and Career Orientation," *Sociology and Social Research*, 50 (1966) 280–95.

————. "Social Mobility and Social Isolation: A Test of Sorokin's Dissociative Hypothesis," *American Sociological Review*, 32 (1967) 237–53.

Emerson, Richard. "Power-Dependence Relations," *American Sociological Review*, 27 (1962) 31–41.

Empey, LaMar, and Jerome Rabow. "The Provo Experiment in Delinquency Rehabilitation," *American Sociological Review*, 26 (1961) 679–95.

Epstein, Lenore. "The Income Position of the Aged," in Harold Orbach and Clark Tibbitts (eds.), *Aging and the Economy* (Ann Arbor: University of Michigan Press, 1963) 91–102.

Erbe, William. "Social Involvement and Political Activity," *American Sociological Review*, 29 (1964) 198–215.

Evan, William. "Cohort Analysis of Survey Data," *Public Opinion Quarterly*, 23 (1959) 63–72.

————. "Peer-Group Interaction and Organizational Socialization," *American Sociological Review*, 28 (1963) 436–40.

Festinger, Leon. *A Theory of Cognitive Dissonance* (Evanston: Row, Peterson, 1957).

Filer, Richard, and Desmond O'Connell. "Motivation of Aging Persons," *Journal of Gerontology*, 19 (1964) 15–22.

Foote, Nelson. "Identification as the Basis for a Theory of Motivation," *American Sociological Review*, 16 (1951) 14–21.

Foskett, John. "Social Structure and Social Participation," *American Sociological Review*, 20 (1955) 431–38.

Freeman, Howard, Edwin Novak, and Leo Reeder. "Correlates of Membership in Voluntary Associations," *American Sociological Review*, 22 (1957) 528–33.

Garabedian, Peter. "Social Roles and Processes of Socialization in the Prison Community," *Social Problems*, 11 (Fall, 1963) 139–52.

Garfinkel, Harold. "Conditions of Successful Degradation Ceremonies," *American Journal of Sociology*, 61 (1956) 420–24.

Ginzberg, Raphael. "The Negative Attitude toward the Elderly," *Geriatrics*, 7 (1952) 297–302.

Glaser, Barney, and Anselm Strauss. "Awareness Contexts and Social

Interaction," *American Sociological Review*, 29 (1964) 669–79.

————. "Temporal Aspects of Dying as a Non-Scheduled Status Passage," *American Journal of Sociology*, 71 (1965) 48–59.

Glick, Paul. "The Family Cycle," *American Sociological Review*, 12 (1947) 164–74.

Goffman, Erving. "Alienation from Interaction," *Human Relations*, 10 (1957) 47–60.

————. *The Presentation of Self in Everyday Life* (New York: Anchor Books, 1959).

Golde, Peggy, and Nathan Kogan. "A Sentence Completion Procedure for Assessing Attitudes toward Old People," *Journal of Gerontology*, 14 (1959) 355–63.

Goode, William. *After Divorce* (Glencoe: Free Press, 1956).

————. "Norm Commitment and Conformity to Role-Status Obligations," *American Journal of Sociology*, 66 (1960) 246–58.

————. "A Theory of Role Strain," *American Sociological Review*, 25 (1960) 483–96.

Goodstein, Leonard. "Personal Adjustment Factors and Retirement," *Geriatrics*, 17 (1962) 41–45.

Gordon, Margaret. "Aging and Income Security," in Clark Tibbitts (ed.), *Handbook of Social Gerontology* (Chicago: University of Chicago Press, 1960), 208–60.

————. "The Older Worker and Hiring Practices," *Monthly Labor Review*, 82 (1959) 1198–1205.

————. "Work and Patterns of Retirement," in Robert Kleemeier (ed.), *Aging and Leisure* (New York: Oxford University Press, 1961), 15–53.

Goslin, David (ed.). *Handbook of Socialization Theory and Research* (Chicago: Rand McNally, 1969).

Grosser, George. "The Role of Informal Inmate Groups in Change of Values," *Children*, 5 (1958) 25–29.

Harlan, William. "Meaning of Economic Security to Older Persons," *Transactions of the Illinois State Academy of Science*, 44 (1951) 182–86.

Havighurst, Robert. "Flexibility and the Social Roles of the Retired," *American Journal of Sociology*, 59 (1954) 309–11.

————. "The Leisure Activities of the Middle-Aged," *American Journal of Sociology*, 63 (1957) 152–62.

Havighurst, Robert, and Ruth Albrecht. *Older People* (New York: Longmans and Green, 1953).

Heilbrun, Alfred, and Charles Lair. "Decreased Role Consistency in the Aged: Implications for Behavioral Pathology," *Journal of Gerontology*, 19 (1964) 325–29.

Hochschild, Arlie. *The Unexpected Community* (Englewood Cliffs, N.J.: Prentice-Hall, 1973).

Hoyt, G. C. "The Life of the Retired in a Trailer Park," *American Journal of Sociology*, 59 (1954) 361–70.

Hunter, Woodrow, and Helen Maurice. *Older People Tell their Story* (Ann Arbor: University of Michigan, Division of Gerontology, 1953).

Hutchinson, Bertram. *Old People in a Modern Australian Community* (Carlton, Australia: Melbourne University Press, 1954).

Impact of Inflation on Retired Persons, National Advisory Committee, White House Conference on Aging (Washington: 1960).

Inkeles, Alex. "Social Structure and Socialization," in David Goslin (ed.), *Handbook of Socialization Theory and Research* (Chicago: Rand McNally) 615–32.

Inkeles, Alex, and Raymond Bauer. *The Soviet Citizen* (Cambridge: Harvard University Press, 1959).

Kadushin, Charles. "The Professional Self-Concept of Music Students," *American Journal of Sociology*, 75 (1969) 389–404.

Kelley, Harold. "Two Functions of Reference Groups," in Guy Swanson, Theodore Newcomb, and Eugene Hartley (eds.), *Readings in Social Psychology*, rev. ed. (New York: Holt, 1952) 410–14.

Kelman, Herbert. "Processes of Opinion Change," *Public Opinion Quarterly*, 25 (1961) 57–78.

Kerckhoff, Alan. "Husband-Wife Expectations and Reactions to Retirement," in Ida Simpson and John McKinney (eds.), *Social Aspects of Aging* (Durham: Duke University Press, 1966) 160–72.

———. "Norm-Value Clusters and the 'Strain Toward Consistency' Among Older Married Couples," in Ida Simpson and John McKinney (eds.), *Social Aspects of Aging* (Durham: Duke University Press, 1966) 138–59.

———. "Nuclear and Extended Family Relationships," in Ethel Shanas and Gordon Streib (eds.), *Social Structure and the Family: Generational Relations* (Englewood Cliffs, N.J.: Prentice-Hall, 1965) 93–112.

Kleemeier, Robert. "An Analysis of Patterns of Group Living for Older People," in Irving Webber (ed.), *Aging: A Current Ap-*

praisal (Gainesville: University of Florida Press, 1956) 167–79.

———. "Environmental Settings and the Aging Process," in John Anderson (ed.), *Psychological Aspects of Aging* (Washington: American Psychological Association, 1956) 105–16.

———. "Moosehaven: Congregate Living in a Community of the Retired," *American Journal of Sociology*, 59 (1954) 347–51.

Kogan, Nathan. "Attitudes toward Old People in an Older Sample," *Journal of Abnormal and Social Psychology*, 62 (1961) 616–22.

Kogan, Nathan, and Michael Wallach. "Age Changes in Values and Attitudes," *Journal of Gerontology*, 16 (1961) 272–80.

Komarovsky, Mirra. "Cultural Contradictions and Sex Roles," *American Journal of Sociology*, 52 (1946) 184–89.

Korpi, Walter. *Social Pressures and Attitudes in Military Training.* Stockholm Studies in Sociology 2 (Stockholm: Almqvist & Wiksell, 1965).

Kuhlen, Raymond, and Everett Luther. "A Study of the Cultural Definition of Prime of Life, Middle Age, and of Attitudes toward the Old," *Journal of Gerontology*, 4 (1949) 324.

Kutner, Bernard, *et al. Five Hundred Over Sixty* (New York: Russell Sage, 1956).

Lebo, Dell. "Some Factors Said to Make for Happiness in Old Age," *Journal of Clinical Psychology*, 9 (1953) 385–90.

Leveen, Louis, and David Priver. "Significance of Role Playing in the Aged Person," *Geriatrics*, 18 (1963) 57–63.

Linden, Maurice. "Effects of Social Attitudes on the Mental Health of the Aging," *Geriatrics*, 12 (1957) 109–14.

Lipman, Aaron. "Role Conceptions and Morale of Couples in Retirement," *Journal of Gerontology*, 16 (1961) 261–71.

Lipset, Seymour, *et al.* "The Psychology of Voting," in Gardner Lindzey (ed.), *Handbook of Social Psychology*, vol. 2 (Cambridge: Addison-Wesley Press, 1954) 1124–75.

Litwak, Eugene. "Geographic Mobility and Extended Family Cohesion," *American Sociological Review*, 25 (1960) 9–21.

———. "Occupational Mobility and Extended Family Cohesion," *American Sociological Review*, 25 (1960) 385–94.

Lorch, Barbara. "The Perception of Deviancy by Self and Others," *Sociology and Social Research*, 50 (1966) 223–29.

Lorge, Irving, and K. Helfant. "The Independence of Chronological

Age and Sociopolitical Attitudes," *Journal of Abnormal and Social Psychology*, 48 (1953) 598.

Lowenthal, Marjorie. *Lives in Distress* (New York: Basic Books, 1964).

———. "Social Isolation and Mental Illness in Old Age," *American Sociological Review*, 29 (1964) 54–70.

Lowenthal, Marjorie, and Deetje Boler. "Voluntary vs. Involuntary Social Withdrawal," *Journal of Gerontology*, 20 (1965) 363–71.

Ludwig, Edward, and Robert Eichhorn. "Age and Disillusionment: A Study of Value Changes Associated with Aging," *Journal of Gerontology*, 22 (1967) 59–65.

Mannheim, Karl. "The Problem of Generations," *Essays on the Sociology of Knowledge* (New York: Oxford University Press, 1952), 276–322.

Martel, Martin. "Family and Friendship Patterns of Older Iowans," *Adding Life to Years*, 8 (July, 1961) 3–6.

Martinez, Thomas, "Why Employment-Agency Counselors Lower Their Clients' Self-Esteem," *Trans-Action*, 5 (March, 1968) 20–25.

Mason, Evelyn. "Some Correlates of Self-Judgments of the Aged," *Journal of Gerontology*, 9 (1954) 324–37.

———. "Some Factors in Self-Judgments," *Journal of Clinical Psychology*, 10 (1954) 336–40.

McCloskey, Herbert, and John Schaar. "Psychological Dimensions of Anomy," *American Sociological Review*, 30 (1965) 14–40.

McCorkle, Lloyd, Albert Elias, and F. Lovell Bixby. *The Highfields Story* (New York: Henry Holt, 1958).

Meerloo, Joost. "Some Psychological Problems of the Aged Patient," *New York State Journal of Medicine*, 58 (1959) 3810–14.

Merton, Robert. "The Role Set: Problems in Sociological Theory," *British Journal of Sociology*, 8 (1957) 106–20.

———. *Social Theory and Social Structure*, rev. ed. (Glencoe: Free Press, 1957).

Merton, Robert, George Reader, and Patricia Kendall. *The Student-Physician* (Cambridge: Harvard University Press, 1957).

Merton, Robert, and Alice Rossi. "Contributions to the Theory of Reference Group Behavior," in Robert Merton and Paul Lazarsfeld (eds.), *Continuities in Social Research: Studies in the Scope and Method of "The American Soldier"* (Glencoe: Free Press, 1950) 40–105.

Michelon, L. C. "The New Leisure Class," *American Journal of Sociology*, 59 (1954) 371–78.

Miller, L. Keith, and Robert Hamblin. "Interdependence, Differential Rewarding and Productivity," *American Sociological Review*, 28 (1963) 768–78.

Mireaux, Emile. *Daily Life in the Time of Homer* (New York: Macmillan, 1959).

Morris, Woodrow. "Age Attitudes and Health," *Adding Life to Years*, 8 (March, 1961) 3–6.

Neugarten, Bernice, and David Garron. "The Attitudes of Middle-Aged Persons Toward Growing Older," *Geriatrics*, 14 (1959) 21–24.

Neugarten, Bernice, and Warren Peterson. "A Study of the American Age-Grade System," *Fourth Congress of the International Association of Gerontology*, vol. III (Fidenza, Italy: Tito Mattioli, 1957) 497–502.

Neugarten, Bernice, Joan Moore, and John Lowe. "Age Norms, Age Constraints, and Adult Socialization," *American Journal of Sociology*, 70 (1965) 710–17.

Nydegger, Corinne. "Timing of Fatherhood: Role Perception and Socialization" (Unpub. Ph.D. Thesis, Penn State University, 1973.

Orbach, Harold. "Aging and Religion," *Geriatrics*, 16 (1961) 530–40.

Orbach, Harold, and David Shaw. "Social Participation and the Role of the Aging," *Geriatrics*, 12 (1957) 241–46.

Parsons, Talcott. "Age and Sex in the Social Structure of the United States," *American Sociological Review*, 7 (1942) 604–16.

———. "Revised Analytical Approach to the Theory of Social Stratification," in Reinhard Bendix and Seymour Lipset (eds.), *Class, Status and Power* (Glencoe: Free Press, 1953) 92–128.

———. "The Social Structure of the Family," in Ruth Anshen (ed.), *The Family: Its Function and Destiny* (New York: Harpers, 1949) 173–201.

———. *The Social System* (New York: Free Press, 1951).

Parsons, Talcott, and Edward Shils. "Values, Motives and Systems of Action," in Talcott Parsons and Edward Shils (eds.), *Toward a General Theory of Action* (Cambridge: Harvard University Press, 1951) 3–29.

Payne, Raymond. "Some Theoretical Approaches to the Sociology of Aging," *Social Forces*, 38 (1960) 359–62.

Payne, S. "The Cleveland Survey of Retired Men," *Personnel Psychology*, 6 (1953) 81–110.

Pearlin, Leonard. "Alienation from Work," *American Sociological Review*, 27 (1962) 314–26.

Phillips, Bernard. "A Role Theory Approach to Adjustment in Old Age," *American Sociological Review*, 22 (1957) 212–17.

Phillips, Derek. "Rejection: A Possible Consequence of Seeking Help for Mental Disorders," *American Sociological Review*, 28 (1963) 963–72.

————. "Social Participation and Happiness," *American Journal of Sociology*, 72 (1967) 479–88.

Pollak, Otto. "Conservatism in Later Maturity and Old Age," *American Sociological Review*, 8 (1943) 175–79.

Prasad, Benjamin S. "The Retirement Postulate of the Disengagement Theory," *Gerontologist*, 4 (1964) 20–23.

Preston, Caroline, and Karen Gudiksen. "A Measure of Self-Perception Among Older People," *Journal of Gerontology*, 21 (1966) 63–71.

Putney, Snell, and Russell Middleton. "Ethical Relativism and Anomia," *American Journal of Sociology*, 67 (1962) 430–38.

Rapoport, Robert, Rhona Rapoport and Irving Rosow. *Community as Doctor* (London: Tavistock, 1960).

Reeder, Leo, George Donahue and Arturo Biblarz. "Conceptions of Self and Others," *American Journal of Sociology*, 66 (1960) 153–59.

Riesman, David. "Some Clinical and Cultural Aspects of Aging," *American Journal of Sociology*, 59 (1954) 379–83.

Riley, Matilda, and Anne Foner, *Aging and Society, Volume One: An Inventory of Research Findings* (New York: Russell Sage Foundation, 1968).

Riley, Matilda, Anne Foner, Beth Hess, and Marcia Toby, "Socialization for the Middle and Later Years," in David Goslin (ed.), *Handbook of Socialization Theory and Research* (Chicago: Rand McNally, 1969) 951–82.

Roland, Warren. "Cultural, Personal and Situational Roles," *Sociology and Social Research*, 34 (September–October, 1949) 104–11.

Rose, Arnold. "Alienation and Participation: A Comparison of Group Leaders and the 'Mass,'" *American Sociological Review*, 27 (1962) 834–38.

————. "Class Differences Among the Elderly: A Research Report," *Sociology and Social Research*, 50 (1966) 356–60.

————. "Group Consciousness Among the Aging," in Arnold Rose and Warren Peterson (eds.), *Older People and their Social World* (Philadelphia: F. A. Davis, 1965) 19–36.

————. "The Impact of Aging on Voluntary Associations," in Clark Tibbitts (ed.), *Handbook of Social Gerontology* (Chicago: University of Chicago Press, 1960) 666–97.

————. "The Subculture of the Aging," in Arnold Rose and Warren Peterson (eds.), *Older People and their Social World* (Philadelphia: F. A. Davis, 1965) 3–16.

————. *Theory and Method in the Social Sciences* (Minneapolis: University of Minnesota Press, 1954).

Rosen, Jacqueline, and Bernice Neugarten. "Ego Functions in the Middle and Later Years," *Journal of Gerontology*, 15 (1960) 62–67.

Rosenberg, Morris. "The Dissonant Religious Context and Emotional Disturbance," *American Journal of Sociology*, 68 (1962) 1–10.

Rosow, Irving. "Adjustment of the Normal Aged: Concept and Measurement," in Richard Williams, Clark Tibbitts and Wilma Donahue (eds.), *Processes of Aging*, vol. 2 (New York: Atherton Press, 1963) 195–223.

————. "Affluence, Reciprocity and Solidary Bonds," paper prepared for the Biennial Meeting of the International Society for the Study of Behavioral Development: Ann Arbor, August, 1973. (publication pending)

————. "Forms and Functions of Adult Socialization," *Social Forces*, 44 (1965) 35–45.

————. "Intergenerational Relationships: Problems and Proposals," in Ethel Shanas and Gordon Streib (eds.), *Social Structure and the Family: Generational Relations* (Englewood Cliffs, N.J.: Prentice-Hall, 1965) 341–78.

————. "Issues in the Concept of Need Complementarity," *Sociometry*, 20 (1957) 216–33.

————. "Old Age: One Moral Dilemma of an Affluent Society," *Gerontologist*, 2 (1962) 182–91.

————. "Professionalization of Social Work Students," Final Report to Social and Rehabilitation Service, Dept. of Health, Education and Welfare, 1969.

————. "Retirement Housing and Social Integration," *Gerontologist*, 1 (1961) 85–91. Also in Clark Tibbitts and Wilma Donahue (eds.), *Social and Psychological Aspects of Aging* (New York: Columbia University Press, 1962) 327–40.

————. "Retirement Leisure and Social Status," in Duke University Council on Aging and Human Development, *Proceedings of Seminars, 1965–1969* (Durham, N.C.: Duke University Center for the Study of Aging and Human Development, 1969) 249–57.

————. "Situational Forces in Adult Socialization" (unpublished manuscript).

————. "The Social Context of the Aging Self," *Gerontologist*, 13 (Spring, 1973) 82–87.

————. *Social Integration of the Aged* (New York: Free Press, 1967).

Rossi, Alice. "Equality Between the Sexes: An Immodest Proposal," *Daedalus*, 93 (1964) 607–52.

Rusalem, Herbert. "Deterrents to Vocational Disengagement Among Older Disabled Workers," *Gerontologist*, 3 (1963) 64–68.

Sarbin, Theodore, "Notes on the Transformation of Social Identity," in L. M. Roberts, N. S. Greenfield and M. H. Miller (eds.), *Comprehensive Mental Health* (Madison: University of Wisconsin Press, 1968) 97–115.

Sarbin, Theodore, and Vernon Allen, "Role Theory," in Gardner Lindzey and Elliot Aronson (eds.), *Handbook of Social Psychology*, second edition, vol. 1 (Reading, Mass.: Addison-Wesley, 1968) 488–567.

Saville, Lloyd. "Flexible Retirement," in Juanita Kreps (ed.), *Employment, Income and Retirement Problems of the Aged* (Durham: Duke University Press, 1963) 140–77.

Schaie, K.W. "The Effect of Age on a Scale of Social Responsibility," *Journal of Social Psychology*, 50 (1959) 221–24.

Scheff, Thomas. "Towards a Sociological Model of Consensus," *American Sociological Review*, 32 (1967) 32–46.

Schein, Edgar. *Coercive Persuasion* (New York: W. W. Norton, 1961).

Schild, Erling. "The Foreign Student, as Stranger, Learning the Norms of the Host Culture," *Journal of Social Issues*, 18, No. 1 (1962) 41–54.

Schorr, Alvin. *Filial Responsibility in the Modern American Family* (Washington: Social Security Administration, 1960).

Sears, Robert, Eleanore Maccoby and Harry Levin. *Patterns of Child Rearing* (Evanston: Row, Peterson, 1957).

Seeman, Melvin. "Alienation and Social Learning in a Reformatory," *American Journal of Sociology*, 69 (1963) 270–83.

Seeman, Melvin, and John Evans. "Alienation and Learning in a Hospital Setting," *American Sociological Review*, 27 (1962) 772–82.

———. "Apprenticeship and Attitude Change," *American Journal of Sociology*, 67 (1962) 365–78.

Seguin, Mary, "Opportunity for Peer Socialization in a Retirement Community," *Gerontologist*, 13 (1973) 208–14.

Shanas, Ethel, and Gordon Streib (eds.), *Social Structure and the Family: Generational Relations* (Englewood Cliffs, N.J.: Prentice-Hall, 1965).

Sheppard, Harold. "Unemployment Experiences of Older Workers," *Geriatrics*, 15 (1960) 430–33

Simmons, Leo. *The Role of the Aged in Primitive Society* (New Haven: Yale University Press, 1945).

———. "Social Participation of the Aged in Different Cultures," *Annals*, 279 (1952) 43–51.

Slater, Philip. "Cultural Attitudes toward the Aged," *Geriatrics*, 18 (1963) 308–14.

Smith, Harold. "Family Interaction Patterns of the Aged: A Review," in Arnold Rose and Warren Peterson (eds.), *Older People and their Social World* (Philadelphia: F. A. Davis, 1965) 143–61.

Smith, Joel, William Form and Gregory Stone. "Local Intimacy in a Middle-Sized City," *American Journal Of Sociology*, 60 (1954) 276–84.

Smith, William, Joseph Britten and Jean Britten. *Relations within Three-Generation Families*, Research Publication 155 (University Park, Pennsylvania: Pennsylvania State University, College of Home Economics, 1958).

Snoek, J. Diedrick. "Role Strain in Diversified Role Sets," *American Journal of Sociology*, 71 (1966) 363–72.

The States and their Older Citizens (Chicago: Council of State Governments, 1955).

Strauss, Anselm. "Transformations of Identity," in Arnold Rose (ed.), *Human Behavior and Social Processes* (Boston: Houghton Mifflin, 1962) 67–71.

Streib, Gordon. "Family Patterns in Retirement," *Journal of Social Issues*, 14, No. 2 (1958) 46–60.

———. "Morale of the Retired," *Social Problems*, 3 (1956) 270–76.

Thompson, Wayne. "Pre-Retirement Anticipation and Adjustment in Retirement," *Journal of Social Issues*, 14, No. 2 (1958) 35–45.

Thompson, Wayne, and Gordon Streib. "Situational Determinants: Health and Economic Deprivation in Retirement," *Journal of Social Issues*, 14, No. 2 (1958) 18–34.

Thompson, Wayne, Gordon Streib and John Kosa. "The Effect of Retirement on Personal Adjustment: A Panel Analysis," *Journal of Gerontology*, 15 (1960) 165–69.

Tibbitts, Clark, and Wilma Donahue (eds.). *Social and Psychological Aspects of Aging* (New York: Columbia University Press, 1962).

Tobin, Sheldon, and Bernice Neugarten. "Life Satisfaction and Social Interaction in the Aging," *Journal of Gerontology*, 16 (1961) 344–46.

Townsend, Peter. *Family Life of Old People* (London: Routledge & Kegan Paul, 1957).

Tringo, John. "The Hierarchy of Preference Toward Disability Groups," *Journal of Special Education*, 4 (1970) 295–306.

Tuckman, Jacob, and Martha Lavell. "Self-Classification as Old or Not Old," *Geriatrics*, 12 (1957) 666–71.

Tuckman, Jacob, and Irving Lorge. "Attitudes toward Older Workers," *Journal of Applied Psychology*, 36 (1952) 149–53.

———. "Attitudes toward Old People," *Journal of Social Psychology*, 37 (1953) 249–60.

———. "Classification of the Self as Young, Middle-Aged or Old," *Geriatrics*, 9 (1954) 534–36.

———. "Old People's Appraisal of Adjustment over the Life Span," *Journal of Personality*, 22 (1953–54) 417–22.

———. " 'When Aging Begins' and Stereotypes about Aging," *Journal of Gerontology*, 8 (1953) 489–92.

———. "When Does Old Age Begin and a Worker Become Old?" *Journal of Gerontology*, 8 (1953) 483–88.

Tuckman, Jacob, Irving Lorge and G. A. Spooner. "The Effect of Family Environment on Attitudes toward Old People and the Older Worker," *Journal of Social Psychology*, 38 (1953) 207–18.

Tuckman, Jacob, Irving Lorge and F. Zeman. "The Self-Image in Aging," *Journal of Genetic Psychology*, 99 (1961) 317–21.

Tumin, Melvin. "Rewards and Task-Orientations," *American Sociological Review*, 20 (1955) 419–23.

Turk, Herman. "Social Cohesion Through Variant Values: Evidence from Medical Role Relations," *American Sociological Review*, 28 (1963) 28–37.

Turner, Ralph. "Role-Taking, Role Standpoint and Reference Group Behavior," *American Journal of Sociology*, 61 (1956) 316–28.

Underhill, Ralph. "Values and Post-College Career Change," *American Journal of Sociology*, 72 (1966) 163–72.

Van Gennep, Arnold. *Rites of Passage* (Chicago: University of Chicago Press, 1960).

Vollmer, Howard, and Donald Mills (eds.). *Professionalization* (Englewood Cliffs, N.J.: Prentice-Hall, 1966).

Webber, Irving. "The Organized Social Life of the Retired: Two Florida Communities," *American Journal of Sociology*, 59 (1954) 340–45.

Weber, Max. *Theory of Economic and Social Organization* (New York: Oxford University Press, 1947).

Weeks, H. Ashley. *Youthful Offenders at Highfield* (Ann Arbor: University of Michigan Press, 1958).

Wheeler, Stanton. "Socialization in Correctional Communities," *American Sociological Review*, 26 (1961) 697–712.

Wilensky, Harold, and Hugh Edwards. "The Skidder: Ideological Adjustments of Downward Mobile Workers," *American Sociological Review*, 24 (1959) 215–31.

Williams, Richard. "Changing Status, Roles and Relationships," in Clark Tibbitts (ed.), *Handbook of Social Gerontology* (Chicago: University of Chicago Press, 1960) 261–97.

Wright, Charles, and Herbert Hyman. "Voluntary Association Memberships of American Adults: Evidence from National Sample Surveys," *American Sociological Review*, 23 (1958) 292–93.

Wrong, Dennis. "The Oversocialized Conception of Man," *American Sociological Review*, 26 (1961) 183–93.

Wulbert, Roland. "Inmate Pride in Total Institutions," *American Journal of Sociology*, 71 (1965) 1–9.

Zborowski, Mark. "Aging and Recreation," *Journal of Gerontology*, 17 (1962) 302–09.

Zola, Irving. "Feelings About Age Among Older People," *Journal of Gerontology*, 17 (1962) 65–68.